21 Days
CLOSER TO
Christ

21 Days

CLOSER TO

Christ

EMILY FREEMAN
with paintings by
SIMON DEWEY

DESERET
BOOK

Salt Lake City, Utah

For
McKinley Oswald and Ralph Freeman,
who tread in His footsteps

"Lift up the hands which hang down,

and strengthen the feeble knees."

—D&C 81:5

Text © 2007 Emily Belle Freeman
Illustrations © 2007 Altus Fine Art

DESERET BOOK is a registered trademark of Deseret Book Company.

Visit us at DeseretBook.com

For more information about Simon Dewey's artwork, visit www.altusfineart.com

Library of Congress Cataloging-in-Publication Data

Freeman, Emily, 1969-
  21 days closer to Christ / Emily Freeman ; illustrated by Simon Dewey.
    p. cm.
  Includes bibliographical references and index.
  ISBN 978-1-59038-802-0 (hardback : alk. paper)
  1. Christian life—Mormon authors. 2. Jesus Christ—Example. 3. Devotional literature. I. Dewey, Simon. II. Title. III. Title: Twenty-one days closer to Christ.
  BX8656.F77 2007
  248.4'89332—dc22   2007021170

Printed in the United States of America
Publishers Printing, Salt Lake City, UT

10 9   8   7   6   5   4

ACKNOWLEDGMENTS

With gratitude . . .

To my parents, Mac and Leslie Oswald, who provided our family with so many opportunities to have personal spiritual experiences and then followed through by teaching us to recognize them. Of all the treasures from my childhood, none are more precious than those moments.

To my brothers and sisters who never tire of hearing the stories that fill up my life. Some of my fondest memories are of the long evenings we have spent laughing around the table after Sunday dinner.

To my husband and children, for their constant encouragement and support. And especially for being so forgiving each time I have said, "I'm almost ready to go . . . I just have to write one more line." In my life you are the parade that I love to sit on the sideline and watch.

To my dear friends and family, for your contribution to this book—but mostly for your contribution to my life. I have been so blessed.

A debt of gratitude to the team at Deseret Book. To Jana Erickson, for reading the words I write and having the ability to bring the ideas to life with creativity that touches the hearts of so many. To Richard Peterson, who was a mentoring friend in my younger years. I am so grateful our paths have crossed again now. To Sheryl Smith, who carefully crafts each page, setting the tone to complement the message. And, to Chris Schoebinger, who dared me to dream.

And finally, I am forever grateful for the countless opportunities each of us has been given to come to know the Lord. Words cannot express . . .

"Thanks be unto God for his unspeakable gift" (2 Cor. 9:15).

The Invitation

If with all your hearts ye truly seek me,
Ye shall ever surely find me.

—*Children's Songbook*, 15

The best invitation I have ever seen came by mail in a large box addressed to my sister. The return address was that of a dear friend. We opened the box and began to lay the contents out on the table. Nestled in beautiful tissue paper, with gold ribbon winding throughout, there was an intricately designed nutcracker, two round-trip airline tickets to San Francisco, and a gift certificate for a three-night stay at a hotel. At the very bottom of the box, on a sheet of fine linen paper, there was an engraved invitation to attend a Christmas party that would last all weekend. It was almost as if she were being invited to Cinderella's ball. Even I was excited for the party, and I wasn't even going. What set this invitation apart from any other was that it came with the promise of a treasure, a journey, and a celebration.

I wish I could have sent this book to you wrapped up in beautiful paper and tied with a gold ribbon, but that would have been a publishing nightmare. Instead, carefully nestled between the covers of this book, you will find an invitation that includes a treasure, a journey, and a celebration.

1

This is an *invitation* for you to take a journey to come to know and recognize more clearly the hand of the Lord in your life. Scattered throughout this book you will find *treasures* that can make the journey more meaningful to you. The *celebration* will come from the moments and experiences that bring you closer to Christ.

Let's begin the journey by quickly unwrapping the book. Most of the chapters

"Behold, and lo, I am with you even unto the end."

—D&C 100:12

include recommended daily scripture study and a reminder to have daily personal prayer. These are two important practices in developing a testimony of Jesus Christ. We can learn much about the Savior as we read of His life and teachings in the scriptures. We can draw closer to Him through prayer. To make these daily moments more meaningful, there are questions at the end of each chapter, which will allow you to assess your own personal journey to know the Lord. Pondering these questions will make the treasure you discover from each day your own. Perhaps these simple moments will become the celebration of your day.

This is your journey, your treasure, and your celebration. Because it is an invitation, you can do with it whatever you like. Maybe you will focus on one chapter every day, or perhaps you would like to read one chapter a week. Choose the way that works the best for you. I hope that what you will receive at the end of your journey is just what you yearn for.

If you begin this process with a humble heart, seeking for a stronger testimony, and come with a desire to truly find the Lord, I believe the Spirit will guide you in the direction you need to travel to find yourself closer to Christ. Remember, these twenty-one days are only the beginning of a journey that will last forever.

May you find joy in the journey, may you have the courage and the commitment to know the Lord, and may His choicest blessings attend you along the way.

"You are embarking on something which is going to take the whole of you."

—C. S. Lewis, *Mere Christianity*, 78

Come and See

THE FISHER OF MEN

Come and See

*Thou shalt see
greater things than these.*

—John 1:50

Years ago, following a particularly long and furious storm, I walked out the front door to assess the damage. My young son Josh who had been terrified of the flashing lightning and the constant pounding of thunder, clung to the bottom of my shirt and followed me outside. As we stepped onto the front porch we were stunned by the most brilliant rainbow I have ever seen. The colors were so amazingly vivid that you could differentiate the breaks between the purples and blues, the greens and yellows, the oranges and the reds. And above this breathtaking sight was a second bow, almost as brilliant and beautiful as the one mirrored below. We stood still, taking it in, and then we began to call out to the rest of the family who were still sheltered inside, "Come and see! Come and see!" This announcement was not good enough for Josh, who took off running across the street and began to knock on the doors of our neighbors. We all gathered to witness the beautiful event that lasted only moments, as rainbows do, and then we returned to our homes feeling blessed to have beheld such a wondrous sight.

Just over two thousand years ago, a similar invitation was given to two men who were fishing. As Christ walked along the shore of the Sea of Galilee, He saw

5

two brothers, Simon and Andrew, casting their net into the sea, for they were fishermen. They said unto Him, "Rabbi, . . . where dwellest thou?" and He said unto them, "Come and see" (John 1:38, 39; see also Matthew 4:18–19). Several other men were given this same invitation, and one of them, Philip, ran to tell his friend Nathanael, who questioned whether or not Jesus was the real Messiah. Philip answered him, "Come and see" (John 1:46).

This simple invitation summarizes the Master's ministry. His was always an invitation: come and see; come follow me; come unto me. He asked His followers to come, and then He showed them the blessings that followed the simple invitation: water turned to wine; loaves and fishes multiplied; the lame walked; the blind saw; the dead would live again. The invitation was always extended. Acceptance was left to the individual. They could do as did the disciples—who straightway forsook their nets and followed Him—or they could continue the journey alone, completely missing the blessing of the wondrous sights they might have beheld.

Today we are given the same invitation that was extended many years ago to the fishermen of Galilee: set aside your nets and come and see. But, will we leave behind our nets, which are so full of other interests and everyday challenges?

We are pulled at on every side by distractions that entangle us. Time constraints, daily chores, work demands, worldly pursuits, pride, or other pressures may prevent us from developing a relationship with Christ. If we are

"My desire today is for all of us ... to have more straightforward personal experience with the Savior's example."

—Jeffrey R. Holland

to be truly happy, if we are to reach our full potential, I believe we must create a place for the Savior in our lives. I testify the sacrifice is worth it. The precious moments that will come as we cast aside our nets will allow us to discover something of much greater worth. As Elder Jeffrey R. Holland said, "My desire today is for *all* of us . . . to have more straightforward personal experience with the Savior's example. Sometimes we seek heaven too obliquely, focusing on programs or history or the experience of others. Those are important but not as important as personal experience, true discipleship, and the strength that comes from experiencing firsthand the majesty of His touch" ("Broken Things to Mend," *Ensign,* May 2006, 70; emphasis in original).

Two thousand years ago, two fishermen left their nets and walked away from everything that would hold them back from coming to know Jesus Christ. Heeding the invitation, they followed the Savior and were blessed to experience incredible events, which burned an undeniable testimony upon their souls. If we are willing, we too can find opportunities that will allow us to come to know the Savior personally.

Learn to listen for the quiet invitation of the Master, the times when He invites you to come and see. Most often this whisper will come as we read the scriptures, visit the temple, attend church meetings, and during the still moments when we sincerely pray. Perhaps you will be led to places in your life where you can come to know Christ more fully. Maybe you will learn how to incorporate His attributes into your character. Hopefully you will come to know and recognize the peace and comfort His Spirit makes possible.

Make this the first day of your twenty-one-day journey. The soft rhythm of sandaled feet might not accompany you, but if you prepare with a prayer in your heart before the experiences of each day, I am confident that the Spirit of the Lord will whisper assurances to your soul that you do not travel alone.

If you want to know who Christ is, come and see. If you need to find answers to deep longings within your soul, come and see. If you are desperate to know the healing power Christ can and will bring, come and see. If you want to become a true follower of the Christ, come and see.

"*If you want to know who Christ is, come and see.*"

The Invitation . . . *Come*

Read the account of the fishermen in Mark 1:16–18 and in John 1:38–39.

The Journey

• Determine what fills your nets. Are everyday challenges such as time constraints, demands from work or home, or feelings of inadequacy or fear holding you back from developing a relationship with Christ?

• Today try to listen for the quiet invitations from the Lord to *come and see*.

Simon Dewey

Come and See
JESUS THE CHRIST

Take His Name

Behold, I will lead thee by my hand,
and I will take thee,
to put upon thee my name.

—ABRAHAM 1:18

Every celebration begins with a time of anticipation. Expectation fills the air as guests gather and mingle, waiting for the host to seat them around a table that has been carefully spread. Little can compare with the pleasure of an evening spent with friends.

This feeling of anticipation surely filled the upper-level room on the evening of the Last Supper. After all that had happened previous to that night, the disciples must have looked forward to a quiet evening alone with the Lord. Entering the room from the dusty, crowded streets below, each would have removed his sandals at the door and found a seat around the table. It was at this moment that Christ taught a powerful lesson that was completely unexpected. Just before supper began, Jesus took a bowl and, after girding himself with a towel, knelt in turn beside each guest to wash his feet. This service caught the disciples by surprise because washing the feet of the guest was traditionally deemed a lowly act, one that only a servant would per-form. As was His nature, the Savior connected this unexpected act of service with a teaching moment: "To share in this washing, was, as it were, the way to have part in Christ's service of love, to enter into it, and to share it. . . . There was deep symbolical

11

meaning, not only in *that* Christ did it, but also in *what* He did. . . . *What* He did, meant His work and service of love; the constant cleansing of one's walk and life in the love of Christ. . . . it is the daily consecration of our life to the service of love after the example of Christ" (Alfred Edersheim, *Life and Times of Jesus the Messiah* [New York: Longmans, Green, and Co., 1899], Vol. II, 500; hereafter, AE).

After performing this sacred service, Christ introduced the ordinance of the sacrament we are familiar with today. "The weekly opportunity of partaking of the Sacrament of the Lord's Supper is one of the most sacred ordinances of The Church of Jesus Christ of Latter-day Saints. . . . We may fail to recognize the deep spiritual significance this ordinance offers to each of us personally" (David B. Haight, "The Sacrament," *Ensign,* May 1983, 14). Just as the washing of the disciples' feet helped them to remember to follow His footsteps daily, the ordinance we participate in each Sunday is intended to remind us of the covenants we have entered into with the Savior. That relationship should be the focus of our everyday life, for the Lord has instructed that "the members shall manifest before the church, and also before the elders, by a godly *walk* and *conversation,* that they are worthy . . . walking in holiness before the Lord" (D&C 20:69; emphasis added).

By partaking of the sacrament we covenant that we are willing to take upon us the name of His Son, and always remember Him, especially in our daily walk and conversation (see D&C 20:77). Think over some of the situations you encountered during the past week. Were your actions consistent with the covenant you have made? Were you able to always remember Him? How did you represent His name?

Each of my children was named after someone they can look up to. My husband, Greg, and I felt just as Helaman did when he explained to his sons Lehi and Nephi, "Behold, I have given unto you the names of our first parents who came out of the land of Jerusalem; and this I have done that when you remember your names ye may remember them; and when ye remember them ye may remember their works; and when ye remember their works ye may know how that it is said, and also written, that they were good. Therefore, my sons, I would that ye should do that which is good, that it may be said of you, and also written, even as it has been said and written of them" (Hel. 5:6–7). Our children enjoy hearing the stories behind their names and the qualities we admire about the person they were named after.

In our home we have a quote from President Gordon B. Hinckley that hangs just above our front door. It reads, "Be true to who you are, and the family name you bear." Shortly after we hung the quote we talked about what it meant to be true to a name. We wanted our children to be reminded every time they walked out of our door that everything they do outside our home represents the entire family. Their choices determine whether or not they bring honor to our family, and also to the person they were named after. Then we talked of another important name that each of us has been given. This is the name of Jesus Christ. King Benjamin said, "Therefore, I would that ye should take upon you the name of

Christ. . . . And it shall come to pass that whosoever doeth this shall be found at the right hand of God, for he shall know the name by which he is called; for he shall be called by the name of Christ" (Mosiah 5:8–9).

Taking the name of Jesus Christ helps each of us to remember Him. As we come to know the Savior through different situations, we might find ourselves remembering Him by different names that endear Him to us. Among others, we may consider Him as a Brother, a Friend, a Healer, or an Advocate. The names of the Savior can become names that we reflect on often, to bring us comfort and calm in times of trial, peace and hope in times of trouble, and courage and strength to always stand as His witnesses. We can concentrate on the meaning of these different names every week as we take the sacrament.

Renewing and keeping this covenant weekly enables us to receive a wonderful blessing. Elder Robert D. Hales explains that when we take "His name and always remember Him and keep His commandments, He gives us the greatest blessing He can give us: that is to always have His Spirit to be with us" ("In Remembrance of Jesus," *Ensign,* Nov. 1997, 25).

Just as the disciples did in the time of Christ, we can consecrate our lives to serve the Lord. It might be in the words we speak, the service we render, or the promptings we follow. Today make it a priority to bear burdens, give comfort, and stand as a witness.

Try to remember Him always.

The Invitation . . . *Covenant*

Read the account of the Last Supper in John 13:4–15.

The Journey

• As you go through this day, find ways that you can bring honor to Christ's name by letting the walk of your life exemplify Him. On this day, try to remember Him always.

• This twenty-one-day journey will introduce different names of the Savior. Every chapter contains one name that relates to a scripture story or gospel principle. Take a moment each day to reflect on how each name describes a way that He blesses your life.

When we take "His name and always remember Him and keep His commandments, He gives us the greatest blessing He can give us: that is to always have His Spirit to be with us."

—Robert D. Hales

Come and See
THE HOLY ONE OF ISRAEL

A Common Thread

The keeper of the gate
is the Holy One of Israel;
and he employeth no servant there.

—2 NEPHI 9:41

In my house there is a keeping room. It is the place where I keep everything that is dear to me. Framed treasures, favorite books, and memory-filled trinkets fill the room. One of my dearest possessions is a copy of a journal written by Greg's great-grandma, Susan Marinda Bullock. She was a renowned nurse, a beloved mother, and a devoted wife. Every January the women in my husband's family gather together to study her journal. While sifting through the stories of her life, we have found a common thread that is woven throughout each page. This thread has helped us come to know and understand the strength of Marinda's faith. Page after page testifies of the power of prayer and the importance of listening to the promptings of the Spirit. Because she is no longer with us, the memories she penned are even more priceless.

Through very simple examples, this journal explains how Marinda obtained her testimony of listening and following the promptings of the Holy Ghost. Her success as a nurse came in part because she would pray before visiting her patients and then listen for the direction that she knew the Spirit would send. Marinda learned to rely on this direction. She recorded many examples of when a mother or child's life had been saved because she had followed those whisperings of the Spirit. Many times, after being faced with a complicated decision, she wrote about how she would go off alone and make it a matter of fasting and prayer as she waited for the answer to come. Her life was filled with adversity and trial. During an especially trying period she writes that a voice spoke to her, most true and tender, "You must be tried, to be proven." Shortly thereafter she wrote, "My Heavenly Father was surely mindful of me. And when we know that, we live our lives free and apart without murmuring with life or the part we are called to play."

This is a woman who had learned to rely on the Spirit in her profession, in her marriage, and in her home. In fact, story after story testifies of her relationship with the Holy Ghost and the miracles that filled her life because she learned to rely on the Spirit. The most powerful entry of the entire journal is found on the very last page. Here Marinda left advice that has been passed down in our family from generation to generation:

> *"To my children and grandchildren.*
> *Learn to listen to the whisperings of the Spirit."*

That is wonderful advice. But her counsel is even more convincing because of the many personal stories she recorded in which following the Spirit resulted in wonderful blessings. Now, four generations later, we are learning from the lessons of her life—how to listen to the whisperings of the Spirit.

President Spencer W. Kimball counseled members of the Church in this regard:

> "We renew our appeal for the keeping of individual histories and accounts of sacred experiences in our lives—answered prayers, inspiration from the Lord, administrations in our behalf, a record of the special

times and events of our lives. From these records you can also appropriately draw as you relay faith-promoting stories in your family circles and discussions. Stories of inspiration from our own lives and those of our forebears as well as stories from our scriptures and our history are powerful teaching tools. I promise you that if you will keep your journals and records they will indeed be a source of great inspiration to you, each other, your children, your grandchildren, and others throughout the generations" ("Therefore I Was Taught," *Ensign,* Jan. 1982, 4).

What if you were to keep a journal of your relationship with Jesus Christ? The pages could contain attributes you admire in Him, lessons He has taught you, or moments when you have felt His love. The journal could become a keepsake of your testimony. Perhaps you would like to start it on this journey closer to Christ and continue it throughout your life. Nephi recorded a promise the Lord gave to him in this regard, "that these things which I write shall be kept and preserved, and handed down unto my seed, from generation to generation, that the promise may be fulfilled. . . . For we labor diligently to write, to persuade our children, and also our brethren, to believe in Christ" (2 Ne. 25: 21, 23).

"For we labor diligently to write, to persuade our children, and also our brethren, to believe in Christ."

—2 Nephi 25:23

Maybe someday, generations from now, someone in your posterity will read through the stories you have recorded and find a common thread, one that will lead them closer to Christ.

THE INVITATION . . . *Keep*

Read 2 Nephi 25:21–26.

THE JOURNEY

• Do you have a written copy of your testimony of Christ? Take time to write one today. You might want to include your belief in Him, your gratitude for Him, or an experience that has strengthened your testimony of Him.

• Obtain and keep a journal of your twenty-one-day journey, recording the treasures and discoveries that come to you as you follow this path.

COME

COVENANT

KEEP

Come and See

THE HEALER

Never Stopping, Ever Searching

The cultivation of Christlike qualities is a demanding and relentless task—it is not for the seasonal worker or for those who will not stretch themselves, again and again.

—SPENCER W. KIMBALL

Sometimes our search to find the Savior can be complicated. We seek Him for direction and advice, searching through the maze of our everyday life to feel His Spirit. Looking back on my life, I realize that the most demanding and relentless moments of the search have done the most to teach me to treasure His companionship. The scriptures are filled with story after story, telling of man's ongoing search to find the Lord. One of my favorites is the story of Jairus, one of the "rulers of the synagogue," whose only daughter was on the verge of death.

With no time to lose, Jairus traveled through the night, never stopping, ever searching to find the Lord. At the journey's end, the distraught man fell at the Savior's feet, saying, "My little daughter lieth at the point of death: I pray thee, come and lay thy hands on her, that she may be healed; and she shall live" (Mark 5:23).

Immediately, Christ set off with the worried father. I am sure the journey toward home must have been just as nerve-wracking as the father's journey to find the Lord. Having left when his daughter was close to death, Jarius's every thought must have been consumed with the hope that his daughter would be alive when he returned. How discouraging it must have been to realize that the journey home would take him down a street thronged with people. The crowd was dense and probably loud. I am sure Jesus moved down the street surrounded by His disciples, determined, just as Jairus was, to arrive at His destination.

In the commotion one woman sat quietly and watched. Suffering from an illness that had debilitated her for twelve years, she had tried all she could to relieve the suffering. Only one option remained, and so she waited. With faith the only thing prompting her actions, she reached out and touched the hem of the Savior's robe at the precise moment He stood closest to her. "For she said within herself, if I may but touch his garment, I shall be whole. But Jesus turned him about, and when he saw her, he said, Daughter, be of good comfort; thy faith hath made thee whole" (Matt. 9:21–22).

In this brief encounter, I imagine that Jairus learned a great deal. This woman had come to know the Savior and therefore had enough faith to know that He would heal her. In her illness she had tried everything she possibly could on her own to resolve the issue—she had seen physicians, she had done all. Through the process she had reached the point where the only relief she could find would come from her faith in the Lord. In this case, "faith had to be called out, tried, purified, and so perfected . . . [because] the thing sought for was, humanly speaking, unattainable" (AE Vol. I, 617). What encouragement this must have brought to Jairus's worried heart, for he also sought healing from the Lord. It was but a small moment, but one that must have had a profound effect on his faith.

The scriptures do not tell us what Jairus did as he waited. But we do know that just after the woman was healed, a messenger arrived from Jairus's house, saying, "Thy daughter is dead: why troublest thou the Master any further?" (Mark 5:35). The father must have been heartbroken to hear such news, but "even these dread tidings of certainty failed to destroy the man's faith; he seems to have still looked to the Lord for help" (James E. Talmage, *Jesus the Christ* [Salt Lake City, UT: Deseret Book, 1976], 314). How could Jairus deny that he had just witnessed a miracle? Perhaps what he had thought to be a detour was part of a process he needed to experience before he could exercise the faith required for his own daughter to be made whole. Christ encouraged, "Be not afraid, only believe" (Mark 5:36).

Upon entering the home, they were met with great disbelief, even laughter, as people mocked the Lord. But Jairus's faith remained firm as he and his wife went with Jesus into their daughter's room and watched in gratitude and wonder as Jesus took their daughter's hand and said: "Damsel, I say unto thee, arise." Imagine their amazement and joy when the young

girl "arose, and walked" (Mark 5:41–42). I am sure the gratitude that overwhelmed Jairus's heart must have brought him to his knees. The demanding and relentless journey had been worth it—his precious daughter had been restored.

Both Jairus and the woman who touched Christ's robe were steadfast in one desire—to become close enough to Christ that they could obtain the miracle they needed. Both, like many of us, realized the desired outcome was humanly unattainable. But they had come to believe that Christ could provide a healing that could not be provided in any other way.

Jairus was relentless in his search to find the Lord. The woman who touched Christ's robe stretched until she received the miracle she longed for. We too can cultivate a relationship with Christ by applying these same principles. Most likely the answer will not come easily. The woman was plagued by her illness for more than twelve years before the answer came. Imagine how trying it must have been for Jairus when, even though he was with the Savior, his situation became worse before it got better. Joseph Smith said, "Whatever God requires is right, no matter what it is, although we may not see the reason thereof till long after the events transpire" (*History of the Church*, 5:135). No matter how long or hard the search, if it brings us closer to Christ, it is worth it. The intensity of the search will make the treasure priceless, one that we will not ever give up.

Our son, Josh, was diagnosed with diabetes when he was three. Dealing with the disease has made the past eleven years difficult. They have been filled with many ups and downs and a lot of discouraging and trying moments. I have spent countless hours pleading with the Lord to lighten our burden. Although Josh has not been healed, I have felt the Savior strengthening both Josh and me to be equal to the task. This year we were asked to participate in a research study. As part of the study, we both took a six-page self-evaluation test. One of the questions asked if we would choose, given the opportunity, to not have this trial in our life, realizing that we would have to also give up all of the learning that had come. Before responding to the question, I sat for ten minutes and pondered all that we have learned, reflecting most on my relationship with Christ. He has lifted me and strengthened me. When I thought I could not go on, He made up the difference. I have come to know the Savior through this journey—and so has Josh.

In the end I determined I could not give that up—it was too precious. This detour, though demanding and relentless, has made me stretch again and again in my search to know the Savior, and that process has led me closer to Christ.

THE INVITATION . . . *Search*

Read the account of Jairus in Matthew 9:18–26.

THE JOURNEY

• Think back on a time in your life when you had to search for the Savior to find strength beyond your own. Try to remember the process you went through in that search. Was it scripture study, more meaningful prayers, or another avenue that led you to Christ?

• Stretch again. Apply one of those principles today.

Come and See
THE LORD OF ALL

Simon Dewry

Who Is This Jesus?

Whom say ye that I am?

—MATTHEW 16:15

It was a room of discovery tucked inconspicuously behind the door at the foot of the basement stairs. My mother called it a root cellar. As a child, I was fascinated by this room. In the midst of winter you could walk through the door and find yourself surrounded by the smell of the damp earth, fresh dirt, and summer. I spent many late afternoons running my small fingers through the clean, white sand and digging up potatoes for our dinner. On one such afternoon, a small magnet that had been in my pocket fell onto the sand. I bent to pick it up and noticed that a cluster of soft black *fur* had attached to the back. I looked closely at the sand where the magnet had fallen, but I did not see any more of the fur there. So I took the magnet, along with the potatoes for dinner, upstairs to my mother to see what I had discovered.

With research we learned that there were particles of iron scattered throughout the sand. Drawn to the magnetic force, these particles clung to the magnet when it fell. Sometimes, when there was absolutely nothing better to do, my sisters and I would go down to the root cellar like gold diggers with pie tins and all different sizes of magnets to see how much iron we could collect. We would drag the magnets through layers of sand and pick up the tiny black fragments, so small that our naked eye would never have noticed them. Although the reward was small, we loved to sift through the clean, black iron in the bottom of our tins at the end of hours of effort.

Years later I discovered a quote from the American preacher Henry Ward Beecher:

> If one should give me a dish of sand, and tell me there were particles of iron in it, I might look for them with my eyes, and search for them with my clumsy fingers, and be unable to detect them; but let me take a magnet and sweep through it, and [it would] draw to itself the almost invisible particles, by the mere power of attraction! The unthankful heart, like my finger in the sand, discovers no mercies; but let the thankful heart sweep through the day, and as the magnet finds the iron, so it will find in every hour some heavenly blessings; only the iron in God's sand is gold (*Life Thoughts Gathered from the Extemporaneous Discourses of Henry Ward Beecher,* ed. Edna Dean Proctor [Boston: Phillips, Sampson and Company, 1858], 116).

At that young age, the iron in the sand was plenty of reward for an afternoon of hard work. Now I am not so easily satisfied. The treasure I seek is the one Henry Ward Beecher has suggested—God's gold. My search is constant, the task both consuming and rewarding. I want to know the Savior.

Over two thousand years ago Jesus walked on this earth. Twelve men and a handful of women were given the opportunity to witness daily the miracle of His life. He told them, "Blessed are your eyes, for they see: and your ears, for they hear. For verily I say unto you, That many prophets and righteous men have desired to see those things which ye see, and have not seen them; and to hear those things which ye hear, and have not heard them" (Matt. 13:16–17). It must have been an amazing experience for those early Saints to see with their eyes and hear with their ears the moments and miracles that had been prophesied, the experiences that those of us who live today only read about. How disheartening and disappointing it must have been for the Savior to realize that "the world knew him not. He came unto his own, and his own received him not" (John 1:10–11). He was like iron in the sand; many were unable to discover His identity as the Savior of the world.

I often wonder how we can prevent ourselves from becoming like that. Can we discover, in every hour, something that will bring us closer to Christ? President Thomas S. Monson has said, "We need not visit the Holy Land to feel Him close to us. We need not walk by the shores of Galilee or among the Judean hills to walk where Jesus walked. In a very real sense, all can walk where Jesus walked when, with His words on our lips, His spirit in our hearts, and His teachings in our lives, we journey through mortality" ("The Paths Jesus Walked," *Ensign,* May 1974, 48).

On one of the Savior's many journeys, He traveled through Samaria and stopped at Jacob's well. I imagine that the day was warm and the city was loud with the comings and goings from such a central location. As Jesus sat by the well, a woman from Samaria approached, and He asked her for a drink. This surprised the woman because the Jews did not normally speak to the Samaritans. She had been taught that she was not good enough to speak to a Jew, and she wondered if this man had misunderstood who she was.

> *"In a very real sense, all can walk where Jesus walked when, with his words on our lips, his spirit in our hearts, and his teachings in our lives, we journey through mortality."*
>
> —Thomas S. Monson

How many of us experience feelings such as hers? Sometimes when we consider having a relationship with the Savior, we may feel we are inadequate; we might question our worth and worthiness and wonder if the Savior recognizes us for who we really are. But herein lies an important lesson—even though Christ was a Jew, He considered this moment with the Samaritan woman of utmost importance because she was of great worth in His eyes. Before He began teaching her, He made her feel valuable. As they talked, Jesus revealed His insight into her life and the problems that she dealt with day-to-day, and she soon realized that He did in fact know who she was. He gently prodded until she finally allowed room for Him in her heart.

What began as an ordinary task suddenly became life changing. As she spoke to the Savior, the Samaritan woman developed a genuine longing for more insight. Who was this Jesus? The quest for knowledge had begun.

We quickly learn that this woman was not completely ignorant. She had been taught that Messiah would come, and she also knew his name would be Christ. Jesus took this knowledge and added to her faith, just as He does with each one of us. As the supreme teacher, He built upon her knowledge, line upon line, until He was able to finally testify that *He* was the promised Messiah. The same is true in our own lives. He will take what knowledge we

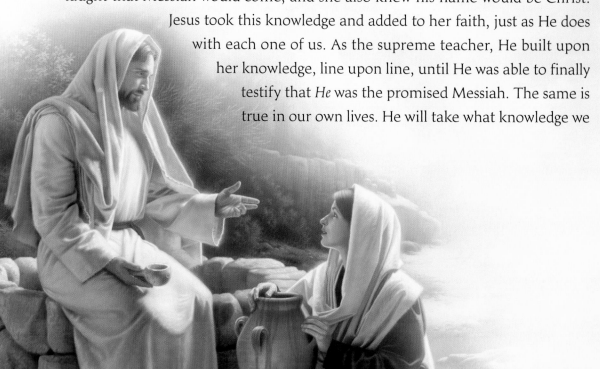

have and add to it until we receive a fulness of knowledge. He knows us. Just as He knew every detail of this woman's life, He knows every detail of ours. And just as He taught her with the simple analogies that were a part of her daily work, He will teach us in ways that we can understand.

For the Samaritan woman, this powerful teaching moment came at a very unexpected time. "She had come—like so many of us, who find the pearl in the field which we occupy in the business of everyday life—on humble, ordinary duty and work" (AE, Vol. I, 408). And it was here that she was taught. Likewise, some of our greatest learning moments may come as we go about our ordinary daily tasks. We must learn to watch for these moments, for these "pearls in the field" of our everyday lives. Then we become true treasure seekers, daily discovering God's gold.

The Invitation . . . *Discover*

Read the account of the Samaritan woman in John 4:1–42.

The Journey

• Prepare to receive a simple learning moment, a "pearl in the field," as you go through your day. Let your search be constant. Try to discover, "in every hour," some heavenly blessing that will bring you closer to Christ. A treasure—God's gold.

Simon Dewey

Come and See
THE HIGH PRIEST OF GOOD
THINGS TO COME

When Hope Is Gone

And so,
after he had patiently endured,
he obtained the promise.

—HEBREWS 6:15

The bitterest times are black. When I look back at the hardest times in my life, the sensation I remember most is darkness. A sense that the world is closing in, the empty feeling of nothingness, the inability to see clearly enough to make simple decisions. That darkness has the ability to shroud the soul, preventing all light from penetrating. In the book of John we read of a man in this condition. This man was blind from birth. He spent every day in the dark. Although surrounded by people, he was completely forgotten and left alone with his trial. I wonder how many times he must have sat in the black world he lived in and pondered his existence. I wonder if at times he even doubted his ability to go forward. Were there days when he questioned everything he had been taught, the reality of God, the beliefs which had sustained him through life so far? I think so.

There is a moment of epiphany after the soul has doubted all it knows, when it begins to reach out for solid answers and firm ground. This moment is defined by one emotion that sustains and creates a desire for change. Before faith or knowledge is found, before joy or happiness is experienced, before the healing begins, one emotion starts to stir from deep within the depths of despair. It is hope. Hope is the light that will begin to lead through the darkest hour, which will enable us to to move forward along the darkened path. It was this light that the blind man sought.

Sometimes this epiphany, this small portion of hope, will bring a change in thought. This change simply helps us to evaluate the situation from a different view than we have previously seen. We are given small portions of knowledge, line upon line, as we work through the abyss.

The blind man experienced this process. The Lord simply changed his point of view. Dust was turned into clay. Simple. And then he was told to go to a place of healing, Siloam, and wash—an ordinary experience that symbolized so much. Wash. Let go, rid yourself of what is holding you back, and heal. The man's eyes were opened. He could see (see John 9:1–41).

There are so many times I have prayed for the Lord to touch my eyes so I might see. In the darkness of the night I have wept and pled for sight, praying that the Lord will help me see the reason for the trial and what I am supposed to learn. I question how long it will be until the trial will finally be over. Sometimes the light is slow in coming, and I wonder if I have the strength to endure. When the reason for the pain is not forthcoming, I turn to the Savior and instead of pleading for answers, I beg for comfort. I remember that during one of the Savior's greatest struggles, Heavenly Father sent unto Him from heaven an angel to strengthen Him (see Luke 22:43). I have learned to trust that in my darkest hours, when I require strength to just exist, He will send an "angel" to help me through.

After spending five long days with Josh in the hospital after he was diagnosed with diabetes, we prepared to go home. We walked out of those hospital doors and into a whole new lifestyle. It was almost as if part of us had died, and with trepidation and uncertainty we faced an entirely new road ahead. Josh, who was three years old, couldn't figure out why he wasn't better since they had allowed us to leave the hospital. He had not anticipated bringing home the shots and needles that were necessary to keep him alive. I will never forget our first afternoon home.

I set Josh up on the counter so I could poke his tiny finger to test his blood and then give him a shot in preparation for dinner. He began to cry, screaming and yelling, "I hate this, I hate you, you don't do this to any of the other kids in our family, why do you do it to me? Why did you ever think I wanted to do this?" I remember he grabbed my cheeks with his tiny hands, pinching as hard as he could. I didn't stop him. When the shot was over I sat down on the kitchen floor and burst into tears. How would we ever get through?

Sometimes a burden will exhaust our energy so much we can't even begin to remember what it feels like to have faith. Although we trust that Christ lives, we may have a hard time believing that we will ever get past the point where we are. There are so many occasions when I have prayed for the Lord to sustain me in a time of trial, to strengthen me, comfort me, and increase my faith and hope to the point that I can begin to heal. I have proved Him, and He has been there.

When the apostles asked Christ why the blind man was blind, He answered that it was for one reason, "that the works of God should be made manifest in him" (John 9:3). Never underestimate the purpose of the trial. The works of Christ will be made manifest in your life. It is through adversity that we experience the sweetest parts of the Atonement. Enduring our trials allows us to experience the healing power of Jesus Christ. This process strengthens our testimony of the reality of Christ and enables us to eventually help lift the hands of another.

President Heber J. Grant gave this sweet promise: "The

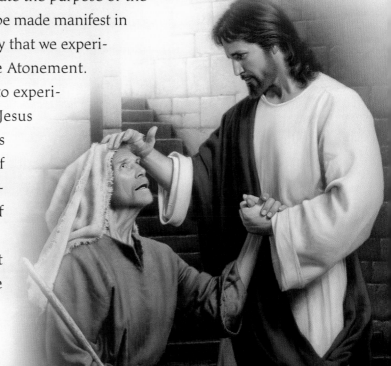

Lord will be always near you. He will comfort you; you will feel His presence in the hour of your greatest tribulation" (First Presidency Message, in Conference Report, Apr. 1942, 96). In the hours of greatest tribulation we can feel the Lord's presence. He will bring us comfort and He will be our strength. Most important, He will give us the hope we need to move forward when hope is gone. Elder Jeffrey R. Holland once said, "On those days when we have special need of heaven's help, we would do well to remember one of the titles given to the Savior. . . . 'an high priest of good things to come'" ("An High Priest of Good Things to Come," *Ensign,* Nov. 1999, 36).

THE INVITATION . . . *Hope*

Read the story of the blind man found in John 9:1–38.

THE JOURNEY

• Attempt to analyze through different eyes a situation that has been troubling you. Pray that the Savior will *touch* your eyes so that you will see what you need to do differently.

• Now take some time to write down some of the *good things* that have come to you through Christ. How does recognizing these blessings bring you hope?

SEARCH

❧

DISCOVER

❧

HOPE

Come and See

THE AUTHOR AND THE FINISHER

A Promise without Parallel

Inasmuch as ye are humble
and faithful and call upon my name,
behold, I will give you the victory.

—D&C 104:82

When I was twelve years old I took up running between two and four miles a day. I loved to run. During those years I ran a 10K (about 6 miles) race each September. I received my number and shirt and lined up on the starting line. My mom and dad would run with me. We would pace ourselves at the beginning of the race, reserving our energy for the end. I remember looking forward to reaching the tables offering water to the runners. I loved to pass one particular curve where I knew family members would be waiting to cheer us on. I hardly remember the fifth mile; every year I barely made it through, and often considered stopping, resting, giving up. At those times my dad would offer encouragement; we would count out the steady rhythm of our stride, and I would match my steps with his, not even looking up as I pushed myself to reach the final mile. When I knew the end was in sight, I would again begin to run my own rhythm, enjoying the feeling that comes when a victory is within reach.

Paul the Apostle has counseled us, "Let us run with patience the race that is set before us, looking unto Jesus the author and finisher of our faith"

(Heb. 12:1–2). Each of us has been given the opportunity to run the race of life. We are given two guidelines as we run the race—to run with patience and to look to Christ. Running with patience suggests rhythm, pacing yourself, and being able to endure. Looking unto Jesus helps us understand we weren't sent to run the race alone. He is given two names as our race partner—the Author and the Finisher. The Author suggests one with authority, who helps us align our course, someone who knows every step of the race and who can encourage us through the journey. The Finisher suggests one who completes and perfects. If we choose to let Him, He will assure that we run the race correctly and that we will be able to reach the finish line. This name is one of comfort. He promises the victory. He will sustain us,, even carry us if need be. He is the Finisher.

There will be times, however, when we will contemplate quitting the race because we can't see the end in sight. We may feel there are pros and cons to giving up early, and we spend the majority of each day weighing each decision. We forget to include our partner and try to find our own rhythm and pace, ending up exhausted and lacking the energy to continue. When this happens we experience pain. We cannot run the race alone. He knows we cannot make it without Him. We are told of things that have happened, the things that are, and the things that will come. He does not leave out any part of the course. But He does offer relief in the form of the strength to endure. He invites us to turn to our Father in Heaven with our needs as we continue the journey. He asks us to pray.

At the end of a general conference session several years ago, President Gordon B. Hinckley set aside his notes and said he would like to just speak with us. Immediately he had my attention. He said he would like to read us a scripture that was the summum bonum of it all. I could hardly wait. And then he read a scripture that I had heard so many times I scarcely listened to the message it contained. That scripture is found in Moroni 7:26:

> . . . Whatsoever thing ye shall ask the Father in
> my name, which is good, in faith believing that ye
> shall receive, behold, it shall be done unto you.

That was it? The summum bonum of it all? I admit I was a little disappointed. During the following week, I read the scripture over and over again. I decided there must be something about it I had missed. I was entirely right.

In Moroni 7:26 we are taught five simple steps to improve our prayers:

1. He begins by saying, "Whatsoever thing ye shall ask the Father . . ." The first step is to *ask.* We must pause long enough to recognize what we are in need of and then ask. The Bible Dictionary explains, "The object of prayer is . . . to secure for ourselves and for others blessings that God is already willing to grant, but that are made conditional on our asking for them" (753).

2. The next step is to ask "in my name," that is, in the name of Christ. We do this because He is our Mediator. We ask the Father for things through Christ because Christ is our advocate; He pleads our case to the Father, giving us a greater chance at the victory (see D&C 45:3–5).

3. The third step is to determine "which is good." Sometimes it is hard to know what to pray for. Our mind wanders as issues become unclear and complicated. We have to do a little research on our own. This step includes a lot of legwork. Many times we can determine what is good only after we have done all we can on our own. Then we can take everything we have learned and place it at the feet of the Lord and ask Him to help us make the decision.

4. The fourth step is to ask "in faith, believing that ye shall receive." It is much easier to have faith when we know the Savior and believe that we have done all we can on our own to receive an answer. There is a moment of silence that precedes this step—a time of reflection. That is when we listen for encouragement; we try to

hear the steady rhythm the Spirit brings; and we match our steps with His, sometimes not even looking up as we wait for direction.

5. The last step is the best step of all: "Behold, it shall be done unto you." Elder Jeffrey R. Holland said, "Some blessings come soon, some come late, . . . but for those who embrace the gospel of Jesus Christ, *they come*" ("An High Priest of Good Things to Come," *Ensign,* Nov. 1999, 38; emphasis in original). The blessings will come. The answers will be forthcoming. We don't always know how, but we can learn to watch for and accept the answers that He will send our way. This watching requires the patience we talked about before. It also requires effort. Not many people can run six miles the first time they take up jogging. And so it is with answers. We learn to receive them, a step at a time, until we become familiar enough with the answers to prayer to appreciate them everywhere around us.

As we become more familiar with the way He answers us, we will learn to pray more often. We will come to expect the answers only He can bring, and we will seek for instruction from the Lord more frequently. "Blessed art thou for what thou hast done; for thou hast inquired of me, and behold, as often as thou hast inquired thou hast received instruction of my Spirit. If it had not been so, thou wouldst not have come to the place where thou art at this time" (D&C 6:14).

After suffering from cancer, my uncle faced a short round of chemotherapy. It was, in essence, an added insurance that the cancer would not return. But after his second treatment things went terribly wrong, quickly. My uncle suffered a severe reaction to the chemotherapy, which threatened his life. I remember the frantic phone call I received from my aunt. Things were looking bad, she said; call anyone you can think of, ask them to pray. She said that during the next twelve hours, things would go one way or the other—he would either pull through, or he wouldn't make it. The news was devastating. I began to pray. I prayed every fifteen minutes for the next twelve hours. Whoever happened to be in the room with me at that moment would kneel by my side. How do you teach your children to pray for a miracle and still trust God's will? Sometimes I prayed alone. I knelt by the couch, next to my bed, in the kitchen. I prayed in the car while driving. I continually poured out my heart to God. And finally, the answer came. Early that evening my aunt called with the news that he had rounded the corner, things were looking up, and he was going to make it. One more time that day my little family gathered together in the family room. We knelt in prayer again. We thanked God for the blessing of prolonging Uncle Dick's life.

Constantly and consistently praying will help us experience joy and the comfort that comes from knowing that the One who knows the path is helping us to finish the course.

THE INVITATION . . . *Pray*

Learn to recognize the steady rhythm of the One who accompanies you along the race by reading Moroni 7:26.

THE JOURNEY

• Ponder the five characteristics of prayer given in this verse. How will remembering these make your prayers more meaningful? Choose one step that you would like to focus on.

• As you kneel to pray tonight, thank your Heavenly Father for His Son, Jesus Christ. Share with Him the reasons why you are grateful for the Savior. Let Him know what your knowledge of Christ means to you.

Simon Dewey

Come and See
THE GOOD SHEPHERD

Recognize His Voice

I am the good shepherd,
and know my sheep,
and am known of mine.

—JOHN 10:14

I come from a long line of shepherds. My father wanted us to understand this part of our heritage, so as we were growing up our family kept a small flock of sheep. One of the sheep I will never forget had the name of "Big Mama." She earned this title because she was the leader of the flock.

Each spring brought changes to the flock as new lambs were born and older lambs would be sold, but Big Mama remained a constant. She loved my dad. It did not matter where she was on the one-acre patch of ground where we kept the sheep, when she heard him call she would come running. She had a very uncommon bleat, and my dad could mimic it exactly. And so he would call, and she would answer, and when she came, the rest of the flock would follow.

One morning my dad woke me up early and said that the sheep had gone missing. They had found a hole in the fence and had wandered off. My dad had already driven through the surrounding streets but had not seen them anywhere. He had concluded that they must have wandered through the fields and joined a flock of more than one hundred other sheep about a mile away from our home.

He wanted me to come with him to talk to the farmer and to see if we could retrieve our sheep.

The farmer was not pleased to see my father. Our sheep were not marked, and unfortunately, neither were his. To him all of the sheep looked exactly the same, with black faces and white wool, and he wanted to know how my dad thought he would be able to prove which were ours. My dad tried to explain that his sheep would come when he called, and the farmer just shook his head.

My dad climbed up on the tailgate of our old white truck and started to bleat. I wish you could have seen the look on that farmer's face. The first and second calls were followed by silence. I have to admit I was a little worried. Our sheep were probably happy to find so many new friends. I wondered how important my dad would be to Big Mama now. But my dad wasn't worried—he kept calling. And finally, from the back corner of the field there was the familiar reply. My dad repeated the call loudly and consistently as Big Mama made her way through the huge flock, followed by our other lambs. The farmer watched in amazement and then helped us load our sheep into the back of the truck so that we could take them home.

In John chapter 10, Christ gave the parable of the good shepherd. To fully understand this parable it is important for us to understand how a shepherd of that time period would care for his sheep. "In the East the flocks are at night driven into a large fold, and charge of them is given to an under-shepherd . . . when the shepherd comes in the morning, 'the doorkeeper' or 'guardian' opens to him. Having thus gained access to His flock . . . the Shepherd knows and calls them, each by his name, and leads them out. Then the Eastern shepherd places himself at the head of his flock, and goes before them, guiding them, making sure of their following simply by his voice, which they know" (AE, Vol. II, 189–90).

Jesus reminded His listeners that a good shepherd, "goeth before them, and the sheep follow him: for they know his voice" (John 10:4). The sheep learn to rely on this shepherd who earns their trust because of his watchcare. He leads them to green pastures and finds them still waters to drink from. He anoints their heads to keep insects away. He protects them from danger and offers healing when they are wounded or ill. He is their guardian, their defender, and their comforter. He makes sure they want for nothing.

Christ said of Himself, "I am the good shepherd: the good shepherd giveth his life for the sheep" (John 10:11). As the Good Shepherd, He has promised to lead us, protect us, heal us, defend us, and comfort us. He gave His life for us. In return He asks each of us to "come, follow me" (Luke 18:22). But to follow Him we must know His voice. In a world filled with confusion and commotion it can be hard to recognize the voice of the Shepherd. Elder Dallin H. Oaks has said, "From among the chorus of voices we hear in mortality, we must recognize the voice of the Good Shepherd, who calls us to follow him toward our heavenly home" ("Alternate Voices," *Ensign,* May 1989, 27)..

The voice of the Shepherd can be heard in many different ways. It may be the still small voice of the Holy Ghost that gently guides and prompts. Sometimes it is the clarion call from the prophet of the Lord, setting a clear standard by which we can direct our lives. Often it is the sure and steady witness of the scriptures that encourages us and increases our ability to recognize the voice of the Lord.

"I am the good shepherd: the good shepherd giveth his life for the sheep."

—JOHN 10:11

To know the voice of the Shepherd is a privilege and a blessing. Setting aside time to listen to the voice is our responsibility. We show our devotion to the Shepherd when we choose to listen to His voice and to come when we are called. His concerned and consistent call will beckon to us daily. It is up to us to quickly answer, "I'm coming!" For "if a man bringeth forth good works he hearkeneth unto the voice of the good shepherd, and he doth follow him" (Alma 5:41).

Sometimes we may find ourselves lost in a world of uncertainty. With so many concerns vying for our attention we may not hear the whisper of the still, small voice, we may not have time to seek out the clarion call, and the sure and steady instruction from the scriptures may be set aside. With time we may find that we are lost. In quiet moments we might feel a silent ache that is masked during the busy flurry of our lives. We might turn to loved ones or favorite pastimes for relief, but in the still moments a longing will remain.

In those tender moments we must remember that there is One who has set aside everything to seek us. He will not rest until He knows that we have heard His voice and we find ourselves nestled safely in His arms. "Is this not the very work of the 'Good Shepherd,' and may we not, each of us, thus draw from it precious comfort? It is not [difficult to imagine] how in folly and ignorance the sheep strayed further and further, and at last was lost in solitude and among stony places; how the shepherd followed and found it, weary and footsore; and then with tender care lifted it on His shoulder, and carried it home" (AE, Vol. II, 256).

The Good Shepherd knows our names and will lead us in the pathway we should go. He knows our deepest struggles and our greatest triumphs. But do we know Him? Do we seek out His presence, go to Him for counsel, and follow the pathway He has marked? How well do we know His voice? How often do we come when we are called?

Find a quiet moment to listen to His voice. How does it speak to you? Try to remember the times that you have found yourself under His watchcare. Reflect on moments when you have been safe folded, led, defended, stilled, restored, guarded, comforted, or provided for. Ponder the blessings that have come into your life because you have answered the call of the Good Shepherd. Looking back through such times in my life, I see blessings unmeasured. In fact, my cup runneth over.

THE INVITATION . . . *Listen*

Read the parable of the Good Shepherd in John 10:1–18.

THE JOURNEY

• Think about how you have learned to recognize the voice of the Shepherd. How has His "voice" come to you? Make a list of the moments when you have heard that voice and have heeded the call. Some ideas may include going to the temple, visiting someone in need, attending church, studying the scriptures, preparing a lesson, praying with a special purpose, or listening to the prophet.

• Find one way to "hear" His voice today.

Simon Dewey

Come and See

THE WATCHMAN

DAY NINE

Ancient Keys

Surely the Lord God will do nothing,
but he revealeth his secret
unto his servants the prophets.

—AMOS 3:7

A couple of years ago our extended family had the opportunity to spend a vacation on a ranch located just outside of Zion National Park. Since we would be staying a number of days, I packed plenty of clothes, and we crammed ourselves into the minivan amongst coolers and suitcases to make the four-and-a-half-hour trip. We had a wonderful vacation, but by the time Saturday rolled around, we were all ready to go home. Caleb, my oldest son, woke up bright and early, begging us to leave in time to make it home for his soccer game. My brother and his wife were leaving early that morning, so we made the decision to send Caleb home with them. The rest of our family would stay until the late afternoon when the others would be leaving.

I quickly helped Caleb gather up his things and then had a brilliant idea: I would send all of our dirty clothes home in a suitcase with Caleb. My brother had plenty of room in his car, and this would give us a little extra space for the ride home. In no time at all they were off, and we settled in for a final day of fishing, canoeing, and four-wheeling. Then we cleaned the cabin, packed the car, and by late afternoon we were ready to leave. Everyone loaded their belongings into the

53

car, climbed into their seats, and settled down for the drive home. As my husband, Greg, was hauling out the last load of garbage, he yelled to me, "Make sure the keys are in the ignition." I checked, but they weren't there. Next he asked me to check under the seat. Again I checked, but they weren't there, either. As he came back around the cabin, he patted his pockets and then said, "Oh, I know where they are, they're in the pockets of the pants I was wearing yesterday."

My heart sank. That meant they were in the pile of clothes I had sent home with Caleb hours earlier. All of a sudden I wasn't as brilliant as I had originally thought. As remote as the area was, I figured we probably couldn't count on FedEx, and I found myself wishing you could email objects over the Internet.

After the initial panic wore off, Greg called a very loyal friend who agreed to drive the keys back down to us. But as I sat there in the middle of nowhere and watched the rest of my extended family drive away, I couldn't help but feel abandoned.

"Great temporal and spiritual strength

flows from following those who have the keys

of the kingdom of God in our time."

—JAMES E. FAUST

I can't tell you how happy I was at midnight when our friend finally pulled up, pushing the electronic button on the keychain that made the headlights on our car flash on and off. I have never been so happy to see a set of keys!

When Christ was on the earth, He held the keys of the priesthood. He promised these keys to Peter, saying, "And I will give unto thee the keys of the kingdom of heaven: and whatsoever thou shalt bind on earth shall be bound in heaven: and whatsoever thou shalt loose on earth shall be loosed in heaven" (Matt. 16:19). These same keys were given to Joseph Smith by Peter, James, and John and have been conferred on every prophet who has served since that time. These keys allow our prophet to exercise "the same divine priesthood power and authority that was held anciently" (David B. Haight, "The Keys of the Kingdom," *Ensign*, Nov. 1980, 73).

If we want to know the Savior, we can look to the prophet who holds the keys and who will lead us closer to Christ. President James E. Faust has said, "Great temporal and spiritual strength flows from following those who have the keys of the kingdom of God in our time" ("The Keys That Never Rust," *Ensign*, Nov. 1994, 74). Throughout the ages the Lord has revealed sacred truths to his prophets. This knowledge has helped many weary travelers find their way back home.

In the Book of Mormon, Mosiah tells of a remarkable time when all of the people came together to listen to King Benjamin. They gathered as families, each pitching their tent to face the direction where the prophet of the Lord would be speaking. So vast was the multitude that they could not all hear him, and King Benjamin "caused that the words which he spake should be written and sent forth among those that were not under the sound of his voice, that they might also receive his words" (Mosiah 2:8). It was a Book of Mormon–style general conference. In his conference address, King Benjamin gave five items of counsel that will help us apply the words of the prophet in our life. These five items are found in chapters two through five of Mosiah.

The first is to "open your ears that ye may hear" (Mosiah 2:9). This is an invitation to take the time to listen to the prophet. We can hear the prophet speak at least twice a year at general conference. This event must become an occasion that we look forward to and plan for.

When I was growing up, our family looked forward to general conference the same way we anticipated an upcoming holiday. We knew it meant two days of relaxation with a lot of good food and no distractions. Throughout the sessions we gathered together to listen to the prophet and the apostles speak. In between sessions there were fun games, long walks, and an amazing omelette brunch to look forward to. I learned to love general conference because twice a year my parents created an experience we looked forward to. Just as the people of King Benjamin set up a tent facing the tower where he would speak, we need to make general conference a focal point in our life.

Second, King Benjamin reminds us to open "your hearts that ye may understand" (Mosiah 2:9). Sometimes we will hear counsel that we do not understand. We can pray that our hearts will be opened to receive new understanding. Then the Spirit can whisper a confirmation that what we have heard is true. It is important to receive our own witness. This is what set Nephi apart from Laman and Lemuel. Even though they all three listened to their father, the prophet, only Nephi prayed to receive a witness that the words his father spoke were true.

Third, we need to open our minds "that the mysteries of God may be unfolded to [our] view" (Mosiah 2:9). For me this includes study. We can look forward to the May and November issues of the *Ensign*, in which the conference talks are published. It is important to reread each of the talks, but particularly those that might have especially touched you. Study these talks and ponder how you can apply the principles in your life.

The fourth item is to remember the words we have been taught. This is not easy to do. After hearing so many words of counsel, it is sometimes hard to remember everything we have learned. I recommend tyring to identify and apply one principle at a time. Write it down and stick it on your fridge or mirror until it is committed to memory. Then move on to another principle. Sometimes it might take the entire six months between conferences just to learn one principle. Other times you might be able to work on a different piece of counsel every month.

The fifth step is found in Mosiah 4:10: "And now, if you believe all these things see that ye do them." Once we have listened with our ears, come to understand in our hearts, studied it out in our minds, and learned to remember the counsel, we need to apply that direction in our life.

The result of doing these things will be to experience a mighty change, which will enable us to come to know Christ more fully. This mighty change will come as we learn to hear and know His voice. By following the counsel we receive from the prophet we can become more like the Savior.

At the close of one recent general conference, President Gordon B. Hinckley counseled us to gather our children and talk about some of the things we had heard. He suggested that we should write down some of these things, reflect on them, and put them into practice. Following that counsel can become part of our general conference traditions.

Our prophet is the watchman on the tower and the man who holds the keys that can lead us safely home. As I look back over the past several years I recall some of the counsel we have been given by President Gordon B. Hinckley: To stand a little taller and to reach out and help those who are in need. He has raised his voice in support of being self-reliant, getting out of debt, and practicing principles of thrift. He has testified of the blessings of paying an honest tithe and has taught the importance of attending the house of the Lord more frequently. Under his watch-care we have been taught to work harder to retain converts, pray more fervently, treat our children with greater kindness, and demonstrate more loyalty and respect for our eternal companions. He reminds us to be grateful, to be smart, to be clean, to be true, to be humble, and to be prayerful. By his very presence and by the things he has said, he has taught us to find peace in a world of uncertainty. He has also instructed us that "it is the opportunity, it is the responsibility of every man and woman in this Church to obtain . . . a conviction of the truth of this great latter-day work and of those who stand at its head, even the Living God and the Lord, Jesus Christ" ("Testimony," *Ensign*, May 1998, 70–71).

I am so grateful for a living prophet who exemplifies these teachings himself and has testified of these things. His conviction has strengthened my belief.

THE INVITATION . . . *Follow*

Read the account of King Benjamin's address in Mosiah 2 and focus on verses 5–6.

THE JOURNEY

• What counsel do you remember most from the last general conference? Glance through the *Ensign* or visit www.lds.org to help you recall some of your favorite talks.

• Write down the counsel given and place it somewhere that you will see it often. How can following that counsel strengthen your testimony of Jesus Christ?

• What is one way you can apply inspired counsel to your life today?

PRAY

❧

LISTEN

❧

FOLLOW

Simon Dewey

Come and See
THE CAPTAIN

Stand

We are living in a part of the universe
occupied by the rebel.
Enemy-occupied territory
—that is what this world is.

—C. S. LEWIS, *MERE CHRISTIANITY*, 45–46

History is replete with wars and rumors of wars. In our day the news is overflowing with stories of combat and contention raging throughout the world. There is a price to pay for liberty, and in our country, all give something. But each of us knows a family who has lost a loved one in the fight for freedom. In that case we are reminded that some give everything.

The Fourth of July is one of my favorite holidays. It gives us an opportunity not only to celebrate the founding of our nation but also to remember those who have paid the price for our freedom. I remember going to a fireworks show the summer following the horrible events of September 11. Music played loudly in the outdoor amphitheater as we watched an amazing array of light dancing high above our heads. We were lying on our backs, with hundreds of families surrounding us, feeling the deep vibration each time a new shower of color burst above us. Toward the end of the show a familiar song came through the loudspeakers, "Oh say, can you see, by the dawn's early light, What so proudly we hailed at the twilight's last gleaming . . ." All around us people began to stand, as is the custom when the national anthem is played. You could hear parents urging their children, "Get up!

Get up!" And soon the entire crowd was on its feet, gazing at the celebration in the sky, considering what it means to be free.

Along with the battles that rage throughout the world today, there is a spiritual war being fought in Zion. President Ezra Taft Benson explained, "There has never been more expected of the faithful in such a short period of time than there is of us. Never before on the face of this earth have the forces of evil and the forces of good been so well organized. Now is the great day of the devil's power. But now is also the great day of the Lord's power. . . . Each day the forces of evil and the forces of good enlist new recruits. Each day we personally make many decisions showing the cause we support. The final outcome is certain—the forces of righteousness will win. But what remains to be seen is *where* each of us personally, now and in the future, will stand in this battle—and *how tall* we will stand. . . . We will never have a better opportunity to be valiant in a more crucial cause than in the battle we face today. . . . Christ . . . is the most successful warrior that ever walked the earth, and He wants to help us win every battle" ("In His Steps," *Ensign,* Sept. 1988, 2).

Those who serve in our nation's military regularly meet with a captain who gives needed direction. The soldiers show their respect to this officer by standing "at attention" while he speaks to them. It is common when the commander is finished talking for him to tell his men to stand "at ease." There is an interesting parallel to this common practice that can be found in our scriptures. As our Captain in this battle, Christ asks us to stand "at attention" in many different ways. We have been instructed to:

Stand by faith (Rom. 11:20)
Stand fast in the faith (1 Cor. 16:13)
Stand and testify (Alma 5:44)
Stand spotless (3 Ne.27:20)

Stand in the place of our stewardship (D&C 42:53)

Stand in holy places (D&C 45:32)

Stand as witnesses (Mosiah 18:9)

Take upon us the Lord's whole armor, that we may be able to stand (D&C 27:15)

Having done all, to stand for truth, righteousness, peace, and faith (Eph. 6:13)

The Lord also gives us a caution, saying, "Woe to them that are *at ease* in Zion" (Amos 6:1; emphasis added). In this fight, we do not have the luxury of "standing down," for as John the Beloved warned: "And the [adversary] was wroth with the woman, and went to make war with the remnant of her seed, which keep the commandments of God, and have the testimony of Jesus Christ" (Rev. 12:17).

One of our greatest strengths comes from *knowing* our Captain. Our relationship must never become stagnant; our communications must never become delayed. "We must know Christ better than we know him; we must remember him more often than we remember him; we must serve him more valiantly than we serve him" (Howard W. Hunter, "What Manner of Man Ought Ye to Be?" *Ensign,* May 1994, 64). In doing so we will become fully converted and able to fight for what we believe.

President Ezra Taft Benson has said that people who are "captained by Christ will be consumed in Christ. . . . Not only would they die for the Lord, but more important they want to live for Him. Enter their homes, and the pictures on their walls, the books on their shelves, the music in the air, their words and acts reveal them as Christians" ("Born of God," *Ensign,* Nov. 1985, 6–7).

Full conversion means that we have complete reliance on our Savior. Toward the end of Christ's earthly ministry, He cautioned Peter, "Simon, Simon, behold, Satan hath desired to have you, that he may sift you as wheat." But then He quickly encouraged, "I have prayed for thee, that thy faith fail not: and when thou art converted, strengthen thy brethren" (Luke 22:31–32).

As our Captain, the Lord will do the same for us. I believe that He prays for each of us, that our faith will not fail, that we will remain strong in the fight. He will watch over us and strengthen us so that we, too, may become fully converted. Then, as our part in the battle that is raging every day, we are to strengthen those around us.

> In ev'ry condition—in sickness, in health,
>
> In poverty's vale or abounding in wealth,
>
> At home or abroad, on the land or the sea—
>
> As thy days may demand . . . so thy succor shall be.
>
> Fear not, I am with thee; oh, be not dismayed,
>
> For I am thy God and will still give thee aid.
>
> I'll strengthen thee, help thee, *and cause thee to stand,*
>
> Upheld by my righteous . . . omnipotent hand.
>
> —*HYMNS,* NO. 85; EMPHASIS ADDED

The Invitation . . . *Stand*

Read Luke 22:31–32.

The Journey

• When you see the battle raging, where do you see yourself in the fight? Consider your church calling, your role as a parent, or your role as a friend. Do you give some, or do you give all?

• Find one way that you can strengthen someone today.

Come and See
THE PRINCE OF PEACE

Calm the Storm

Seek the Lord . . .
[for] he be not far from every one of us.

—Acts 17:27

Late one evening the disciples found themselves aboard a ship in the midst of the sea. The wind was contrary, and as they approached the darkest hours of the night they were tossed with waves. Surrounded by the stormy water and howling wind, turbulent enough that none were able to sleep, they were filled with fear. While suffering these afflictions, they looked up and saw Christ walking on the sea. He quickly assured them, "Be of good cheer; it is I; be not afraid." And Peter answered Him and said, "Lord, if it be thou, bid me come unto thee on the water." "Christ's answer was as it always is every time: 'Come'" (see Matt. 14:27–28), said Elder Jeffrey R. Holland.

Instantly, as was his nature, Peter sprang over the vessel's side. In this defining moment we are shown the character of Peter and the magnitude of his faith. In his desire to come unto Christ he willingly left the safety of the ship and stepped out onto the churning water. "While his eyes were fixed upon the Lord, the wind could toss his hair and the spray could drench his robes, but all was well—he was coming to Christ." But Peter was quickly distracted. He realized the force of the elements around him; he felt the boisterous wind and saw the turbulent waters;

and he became afraid and began to sink. "It was only when his faith wavered and fear took control, only when he removed his glance from the Master to look at the furious waves and the ominous black gulf beneath, only then did he begin to sink into the sea. In . . . terror he cried out, 'Lord, save me'" (Jeffrey R. Holland, "Broken Things to Mend," *Ensign,* May 2006, 71).

"We talk of Christ, we rejoice in Christ, we preach of Christ . . . that our children may know to what source they may look."

—2 NEPHI 25:26

The important part of this story is that when Peter cried unto the Lord, Christ was there immediately. Jesus stretched forth His hand and caught him.

Many times we find ourselves in a similar situation. We become overwhelmed with the magnitude of the path before us. Questioning our ability to move forward, we begin doubting our ability to go on. And so the storm begins to churn within. We find ourselves faltering, sinking, losing the ability to believe. We wonder if the Lord will carry us through our own raging waters, if He will stretch forth His hand and catch us. Peter's mistake was taking his eyes off the Savior and letting the raging of the world around him become his focus. So often in the process of learning we take *our* eyes off the Savior. We lose sight of the goal and find ourselves focusing instead on the turmoil that surrounds us, losing faith that He is able to calm the storm.

Distractions come quickly in the busy world we live in. Sometimes the pressure comes from discouragement or depression that can somehow turn our lives upside down. Often we find ourselves caught in a whirlwind of demands and time constraints that do not allow us to focus on the Lord. Finding time to pray and have daily scripture study always sounds so simple when suggested in a Sunday School lesson. But how do we fit it into our real-life situations? Sometimes the simplest tasks are the ones that become forgotten first.

An important step in coming closer to Christ is finding time to focus on the Lord daily. One of my favorite scriptures is found in 2 Nephi, chapter 25. In this chapter Nephi gives specific advice on how we can remain focused on the Savior. In verse 26 he says, "We talk of Christ, we rejoice in Christ, we preach of Christ . . . that our children may know *to what source they may look*" (2 Ne.25:26; emphasis added). When I am analyzing my relationship with Christ, I turn to this verse. It helps me to sharpen my focus. Not only do I want my children to know to what source they should look, I also want to remember to focus on Christ. Nephi gives us three distinct ways we can look to Christ in our homes.

First, Nephi encourages us to *talk* of Christ.
- Do our conversations with our spouse, our children, even our friends reflect personal experiences we are having daily with the Savior?
- Do we share our testimonies regularly with the people we love the most?

Second, he encourages us to *rejoice* in Christ.
- How often do we take the time to literally rejoice when we receive an answer to a prayer or a tender mercy from the Lord?
- Do we take time from what we are doing to slow down and offer up a prayer of thanksgiving in the very moment when we recognize the merciful hand of the Lord in our lives?

Third, he suggests that we *preach* of Christ.
- How faithful are we in regularly holding family home evenings?
- Do we take the time on Sunday to reflect with our families on what we have heard or felt at church?
- Do we find frequent opportunities to teach about the Savior in our homes?

Individually these practices may seem simple, but combined they can have a profound effect on our lives and the lives of the members of our families. Living this counsel can redefine our focus. Then Christ will become more than just a painting hanging in our homes or a porcelain figure displayed on our bookshelves—He will become a friend. When we focus on Him, Christ will become the center of our lives—someone we long to talk to and someone we long to be with.

In the last chapter of John we find some of the disciples again riding in a boat without the Savior. This time they are fishing. Many things had transpired since the day Peter walked on water. Their faith had been tested and tried. They had experienced miracles and disappointment. Christ had been crucified and then raised from the dead.

Imagine the learning that had taken place, imagine the powerful gift of knowledge these men carried with them—the knowledge that the Savior truly does visit His people in the daily course of their lives. They were true witnesses of Jesus Christ.

They had fished through the night, and when morning came, a man they did not immediately recognize stood on the shore watching. Then "that disciple whom Jesus loved" said to Peter, "It is the Lord," and the disciples began rowing toward the shore to meet the Lord.

But not Peter. In his exuberance, his excitement to be with Christ, he jumped right into the sea and began to swim. His focus was on the Lord. He longed to be near Him. He could not wait (see John 21:1–19).

THE INVITATION . . . *Focus*

Read the accounts of Peter's focus on Christ in Matthew 14:22–33 and John 21:1–19.

THE JOURNEY

• Today remember to focus on Christ. Allow Him to become part of your conversations, your celebrations, your teaching moments, and your thoughts. Long to be near Him.

Simon Dewey

Come and See
THE GIVER OF EVERY
GOOD GIFT

The Gift

Go home to thy friends,
and tell them how great things
the Lord hath done for thee.

—MARK 5:19

One Thanksgiving I will never forget was when I visited the Youth Detention Center in Salt Lake City. This facility is a temporary home for boys and girls ranging in age from eight to seventeen. Most are there because they have committed a crime. Some have been affiliated with gangs. Their days consist of school classes and meals; their nights are spent in a cell. Many of their memories are filled with violence and drugs.

I was asked to speak to them about gratitude on the night before Thanksgiving. It was one of the hardest talks I have ever prepared. When it was time for the meeting to begin, I watched them silently file into the room; each group followed a counselor to make sure they behaved. The young people were not allowed to talk or to make any signals with their hands. As I looked into their faces, I noticed that each seemed set in stone, as if they were determined not to show any emotion. I wondered what kind of lives had led them to this place—how many of them had come from homes that were empty of love or affection? How many of them had been born addicted to a drug they had received from their pregnant mothers? What chance for success could they possibly have?

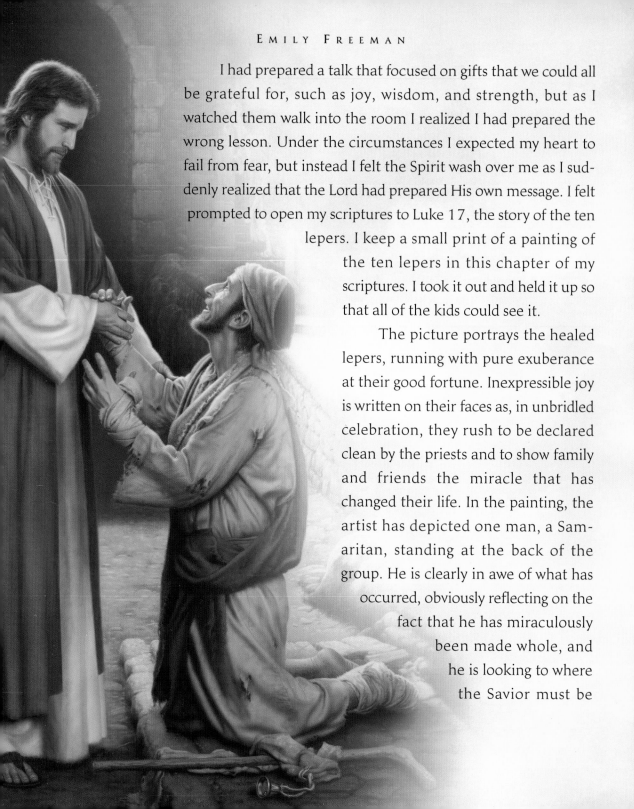

I had prepared a talk that focused on gifts that we could all be grateful for, such as joy, wisdom, and strength, but as I watched them walk into the room I realized I had prepared the wrong lesson. Under the circumstances I expected my heart to fail from fear, but instead I felt the Spirit wash over me as I suddenly realized that the Lord had prepared His own message. I felt prompted to open my scriptures to Luke 17, the story of the ten lepers. I keep a small print of a painting of the ten lepers in this chapter of my scriptures. I took it out and held it up so that all of the kids could see it.

The picture portrays the healed lepers, running with pure exuberance at their good fortune. Inexpressible joy is written on their faces as, in unbridled celebration, they rush to be declared clean by the priests and to show family and friends the miracle that has changed their life. In the painting, the artist has depicted one man, a Samaritan, standing at the back of the group. He is clearly in awe of what has occurred, obviously reflecting on the fact that he has miraculously been made whole, and he is looking to where the Savior must be standing. The scriptures tell us that rather than running off, this man turned back "and fell down on his face at [Jesus'] feet, giving him thanks" (Luke 17:16). In his commentary on this miracle, Alfred Edersheim speculates on how Christ may have viewed this event. He talks of how the Savior must have watched them turn to go: "he may have followed them with His eyes, as, but a few steps on their road of faith, health overtook them." Then he talks of the grateful Samaritan, who, "with voice of loud thanksgiving, hastened back to his healer . . . and in humblest reverence fell on his face at the feet of Him to Whom he gave thanks. This Samaritan had received more than new bodily life and health: he had found spiritual healing." Edersheim goes on to explain that it was one thing to apply to Jesus for healing, "but it was far different to turn back and to fall down at His feet in lowly worship and thanksgiving. That made a man a disciple" (AE, Vol. II, 329–30).

Walking up and down among the incarcerated youth, I shared the story of the ten lepers with them and watched their faces soften as they considered the story. Just like the lepers who lived outside the village, completely isolated from society, each of these young people had been brought to this place alone, without friends, family, or anything familiar. Each of their lives was different now. Perhaps this was a story they could relate to.

"If we turn to the Savior and seek His counsel, we too can be healed and given the chance to live again."

Then I spoke to them of the unexpected opportunity the lepers had been given to change. For a leper, becoming clean was an impossible dream, and there was only One who could make it happen, and that was Jesus Christ. We talked about those times in life when we find ourselves in a situation we might not know how to get out of. Unable to solve the problem on our own, we become isolated. Distancing ourselves from what is familiar, we wonder if we can ever return. During times of reflection we need to remember that there is always a way back. We are given the opportunity, any time we choose, to make a life change. That opportunity comes from Christ through the Atonement. If we turn to the Savior and seek His counsel, we too can be healed and given the chance to live again. This healing requires giving our whole heart to follow the counsel of the Lord.

As I talked with the kids at the detention center, I watched them ponder that thought as they carefully studied the picture. I wondered if they could really give up the things that held them bound. Their challenges seemed so massive; could they make the change? How many would have the strength it takes to choose Christ? I couldn't refrain from asking them as they intently searched the picture, "Look at these ten lepers. Of all of them, which one do you think loved Jesus the most?" Out of the silence one boy raised his eyes to meet mine. He pointed to the one who stood still, and whispered confidently, "That one."

One boy had realized the full magnitude of the moment.

It was more than celebrating the gift—it was recognizing the Giver.

The Invitation . . . *Change*

Read the account of the lepers in Luke 17:11–19.

The Journey

• Identify a change that you would like to make in your own life. It could be something amiss in your family, your work, your relationships, or an individual weakness. Write down a plan that will enable you to make that change. Approach the Lord in prayer and ask for His help.

Simon Dewey

Come and See
THE LIGHT OF THE WORLD

Out of Darkness

*Let us walk
in the light of the Lord.*

—Isaiah 2:5

A youngster walking through a dense London fog was carrying a lighted lantern.

"'Guide me back to my hotel,' said a voice from out of the fog, 'and I'll give you a shilling.'

"'Yes, sir.'

"And so the boy, holding his lantern high, started walking in the fog and soon reached the hotel. As he paused, not one man but four stepped forward with a shilling. The other three had seen the light and followed without question. It is so with any who lead the way to truth and light" (See N. Eldon Tanner, "The Power of Example," *Ensign*, Dec. 1981, 4).

It is amazing what darkness can do. It has an unsettling effect, altering our perception and creating a sense of unease. In a recent general conference, I noticed how many apostles alluded to the fact that we live in perilous times. Uncertainty surrounds us and often the dangers that are lurking around us are hidden from our view. The best way to move forward through these perilous times is to focus on the teachings of Christ. Through the scriptures and the living prophet we will be guided in the direction of safety. But is this all it will take for His light to shine through the darkest hours and inspire us to make good decisions?

Isaiah asks, "Who is among you that feareth the Lord, that obeyeth the voice of his servant, that walketh in darkness, and hath no light? let him trust in the name of the Lord, and stay upon his God. Behold, all ye that kindle a fire, that compass yourselves about with sparks: walk in the light of your fire, and in the sparks that ye have kindled. This shall ye have of mine hand; ye shall lie down in sorrow" (Isa. 50:10–11).

"The people that walked in darkness have seen a great light."

—ISAIAH 9:2

This scripture teaches a very important lesson, but it has to be learned line upon line. None of us wants to lie down in sorrow. To avoid that we have to understand what this scripture tells us to do. The first line describes a person who has learned about Christ and follows the commandments from the prophet, but who walks in darkness because he has no light. It seems that Isaiah gave us a contradiction. How could this happen? If we skip down a line, Isaiah makes it clear by painting a very interesting description. He describes a light that is manmade with sparks that the individual has kindled. This is a person who has obtained knowledge, but instead of relying on the light of Christ, has chosen to rely on his own light and strength.

One of the greatest struggles Christians through all time have faced is apathy. Going through the motions won't prevent us from distancing ourselves from the Lord. It is important that we remain focused as to where our commitment and devotion lie. Elder M. Russell Ballard said, "As I read and ponder the scriptures and carefully consider the Lord's counsel to His followers in every dispensation of time, it appears to me that the most important thing *every* one of us can do is examine our own commitment and devotion to the Lord Jesus Christ. We must carefully guard against spiritual apathy and work to maintain the full measure of our loving loyalty to the Lord" ("How Is It with Us?" *Ensign,* May 2000, 31; emphasis in original).

To avoid walking in darkness, Isaiah encourages us to trust in the name of the Lord and stay upon our God. It takes a lot of faith to realize that we can't do everything on our own and then to learn to trust in and be supported by the Lord. It is by doing this that we come to know His will for us. That knowledge will define our actions. When we trust Him enough to accept His will and learn to lean on Him for our support, then we will be filled with His light.

As we walk through one of the darkest times in history we would be wise to look to the Light. Then it will be said of us as it was of the people in Isaiah 9:2, "The people that walked in darkness have seen a great light." That "great light" is Christ. He is the sure and steady beam that will lead us safely home.

The Invitation . . . *Reflect*

Read Isaiah 50:10–11.

The Journey

• Write down some ways that you have been able to turn to the Lord for direction and support.

• Write down some of the ways you have learned to trust Him.

• Today find one way to share your testimony of these two principles with someone who is struggling.

Simon Dewey

Come and See
THE TEACHER

The Better Part

One thing is needful.

—LUKE 10:42

We were on vacation one beautiful November morning, and I found myself wandering through a straw market in the middle of an island in the Bahamas. Although the tent held hundreds of little booths, by the time we walked down the third aisle we were aware that all of the vendors were peddling the same goods. Every booth offered one of five different items—straw purses, lava lava skirts, tiny glass trinkets, rattles, or $5 T-shirts. Squished together, on either side of a very small aisle, the island people who owned the shops would call out, "You want a purse, ma'am, your pretty daughter would like a purse?" And sure enough, four-year-old Grace did want a purse, a purse with a matching wallet to boot! And so we searched up and down every aisle. I wasn't sure what we were looking for—it seemed all of the purses were of identical design, each one boasting a face of one of many different popular cartoon characters, but to Grace, none was right, and so the search continued.

We passed by woman after woman, hand-sewing the identical faces onto the purses. Some even offered to sew Grace's name onto the purse, but still she could not be persuaded.

Finally, after what seemed like a very long time, Grace stopped. She had found what she was looking for: a tiny purse with little pink rosebuds sewn on top and a bonnet and matching slippers to go with it. This was it! We could finally make the purchase.

I knew exactly what to do—this wasn't my first trip to a straw market—I began to barter. The woman had offered her price, ten dollars for the purse, eight dollars for the slippers, and ten dollars for the hat. Because I was buying three items, I knew I had room to maneuver. I offered twenty dollars for the lot. She wouldn't budge! I played along and began to walk away, fully intending that she would call me back, but she never yelled out a larger dollar amount. Finally, I turned around. "I'm not going to buy that purse for ten dollars when I can buy every other purse in this market for six dollars," I told her.

"Go buy the other purses," she said, "You won't find another purse like this anywhere here. I do quality work." The old woman sat patiently in her chair with her wrinkled hands folded in her lap. She was right. I looked down at the purse. It was beautiful and unique. One could see the care she had taken in placing each pink rosebud. And it matched the slippers and the bonnet perfectly. She even agreed to sew on Grace's name. We ended up buying the set for twenty-eight dollars.

The old woman smiled as Grace put on the bonnet and the slippers. As Grace pulled the purse over her little shoulder, the vendor giggled and clapped her hands with delight. I didn't feel one ounce of remorse that I had lost. I was most grateful I had met that woman; she taught me a valuable lesson on self-worth: she knew who she was; she believed in the quality of her work.

How often in our lives do we choose to give the better part? I think of that island woman: every day she wakes up and walks to a hot, overcrowded tent filled with dozens of competitors and sells items crafted by her own hands to a group of travelers who barter to pay a meager sum. And yet, she has found joy and accomplishment in the quality of her work. Every day she gives the better part.

It reminds me of the story of Mary and Martha found in Luke 10. Most often when we hear this story, we are reminded that Mary chose the good part, which shall not be taken away from her. But what about Martha? While Mary sat listening to the words of the Savior, "Martha was cumbered about much serving." It sounds as though she also felt a little sorry for herself, for she questioned the Master, "Lord, dost thou not care that my sister hath left me to serve alone?" (v. 40).

How often do we feel that what we do goes unnoticed or is unappreciated? Sometimes we might even feel taken for granted by those we serve. But we need not wonder if the Lord cares. He cares deeply about each of us. And He loves those who selflessly serve just as much as He loves those who pause to listen to His teachings. In John 11:5 we read, "Now Jesus loved Martha, and her sister."

As we read on through the New Testament and into the last week of the Savior's life, we again find ourselves in the home of Mary and Martha. In John 12:2 it says, "There they made him a supper; and Martha served." I don't think it is happenstance that in two different scriptural accounts we read about Martha serving. I believe that was her talent. I believe it brought her great joy. I believe it was what she did best. In her life perhaps doing the dishes and sweeping the floor, mending the tattered and the torn, feeding the weary and the worn, and simply giving her heart was the better part of all that she had to offer.

Each day we have the opportunity to give the better part. We too may feel cumbered and troubled about many things, but we can take the opportunity to lift and brighten the lives of others by simply doing that which we do best. President Gordon B. Hinckley has said, "I have been quoted as saying, 'Do the best you can.' But I want to emphasize that it be the very best. We are too prone to be satisfied with mediocre performance. We are capable of doing so much better. Brethren and sisters, we must get on our knees and plead with the Lord for help and

direction. We must then stand on our feet and move forward" ("Standing Strong and Immovable," *Worldwide Leadership Training Meeting*, 10 Jan. 2004, 21).

Our Heavenly Father will give us the direction we need as we try to determine what qualities make us unique. Each of us has been blessed with gifts and abilities that are individual to us. With use, these abilities will make a difference in our lives and in the lives of the people we come in contact with. Discovering what we do best will bring a happiness and contentment that cannot be found any other way.

Spend some time in conversation with Heavenly Father. Ask Him to help you recognize the gifts you have been given. Take time to listen for a response. Pondering the following questions might also help you become more aware of what makes you unique.

What motivates you spiritually?

What is one gospel subject that you enjoy studying?

What meaningful activities bring you the most joy?

Which of those activities help you feel closer to Christ?

What qualities do you have that can help others feel closer to Christ?

We do not all have the same gifts or talents. Mary and Martha were very different from each other. We need to learn to celebrate the gifts we have been given and then learn how to be the very best we can in those areas. At different times in our lives we might be given different gifts or qualities that will benefit us or those we serve. Learning to utilize those gifts to the best of our ability is what constitutes giving the better part.

When we know who we are and have identified the qualities and gifts we have been given, the service we offer will be our very best. In a message to the women of the Church, President Hinckley said, "Thank you for being the kind of people you are and doing the things you do. May the blessings of heaven rest upon you. May your prayers be answered and your hopes and dreams become realities. . . . You are doing the best you can, and that best results in good to yourself and to others. Do not nag yourself with a sense of failure. Get on your knees and ask for the blessings of the Lord; then stand on your feet and do what you are asked to do. Then leave the matter in the hands of the Lord. You will discover that you have accomplished something beyond price.
. . . You may never know how much good you accomplish. Someone's

life will be blessed by your effort" ("To the Women of the Church," *Ensign,* Nov. 2003, 113–15).

THE INVITATION . . . *Do Your Best*

Read the story of Martha found in Luke 10:38–42.

THE JOURNEY

• Remember who you are. What are you best at? What gift can you offer? How can that gift bring more joy to the people around you?

• Choose to give the better part today. Find one way that you can use your gift to serve someone else's need.

STAND

꧁꧂

FOCUS

꧁꧂

CHANGE

꧁꧂

REFLECT

꧁꧂

DO YOUR BEST

Come and See
THE GUEST

The Sycomore Tree

The Lord be with us till the night
Enfold our day of rest,
And be in ev'ry heart the light,
In ev'ry home the guest.

—HYMNS, NO. 161

Luke, chapter 19, tells the story of a man named Zacchaeus who hoped to see Jesus when He passed through Jericho. The scriptures tell us that this man held a high position and was quite rich. Zacchaeus was also "little of stature" and "could not for the press" see the Savior. But he was not about to let the circumstances prevent him from seeing "who [Jesus] was" (v. 3). He ran ahead and climbed up into a sycomore tree for a better view.

There he waited and watched for the Lord to come near. "And when Jesus came to the place, he looked up, and saw him, and said unto him, Zacchaeus, make haste, and come down; for to day I must abide at thy house. And he made haste, and came down, and received him joyfully" (Luke 19:5–6).

How many of us frequently find ourselves in a similar situation? We live in a world that moves at a very fast pace. With email, cell phones, and FedEx, our lives are never still. We work longer hours with shorter deadlines. Success today has become more than holding an important position or acquiring wealth; we want the most for our children, our families, and ourselves. Often this means filling our schedules and every spare moment with more and more of what we hope will bring us joy. Somewhere in the press of all of these demands, we try to make room for the Savior. But are we wise enough to take the time and remove ourselves to a place where we can sit apart from the daily grind and allow Him a place in our lives? Walking away for even a moment can help us receive needed counsel from the Lord.

To catch an unimpeded view of the Savior, Zacchaeus had to climb into a sycomore tree. Where is your sycomore tree? Think of a place where you can go, which will allow you unimpeded access to the Lord. Spend a moment there and take the time to prioritize what is most important in your life. In doing so, consider the direction that the Savior gave Zacchaeus: "To day I *must* abide at thy house" (Luke 19:5; emphasis added). That guidance is just as important for each one of us. The Savior's Spirit *must* abide in our homes every day, but it is up to us to decide how, or even if, we will invite Him in.

"Pour out your souls [to God] in your closets."

—ALMA 34:26

The Savior did not suggest that Zacchaeus should stay in that place where he had discovered the Lord. He told Zacchaeus to come down, to come back into the press, and then follow the direction He had given. Likewise, we cannot ignore the responsibilities and pressures that surround us. Being wise enough to remove ourselves for a short time to focus on the Savior will give us the opportunity to move forward with determination in the direction that we need to go. Then we need to come back to our everyday life with a resolution to follow the guidance we have been given. Zacchaeus was told to "make haste" (v. 5) as he prepared for the Lord, and he did. Once he had *come down* there was an urgency, a higher level of priority given to this task than to any other task he might have had. Because of his preparation he was able to receive the Savior joyfully.

Joseph Smith once said, "Seek to know God in your closets" (*History of the Church*, 5:31). Next to the fireplace in the master bedroom of Joseph and Emma's home in Nauvoo there is a small closet. Inside the closet there is ladder that leads up to a tiny alcove. The secret haven at the top of the ladder is just large enough for one person to sit comfortably, and we are told it was a private place where Joseph could go and ponder. I wonder how many conversations between Joseph and the Lord took place there. It seems that the Prophet knew the importance of having a special place where he could escape to find a quiet moment with the Lord.

Today you might not have the opportunity to sit in a tree or climb a ladder into a hidden alcove, but set aside some time to find your own secret haven. Spend a moment there to ponder. Sometimes reaching higher can fill the longing deep within our hearts.

Let that secret haven become your sycamore tree. Go there to seek the Lord, then make haste to prepare and receive Him joyfully.

The Invitation . . . *Be Still*

Read the story of Zacchaeus found in Luke 19:1–6.

The Journey

• First, find your sycamore tree, or the quiet place you can go to focus on the Lord.

• Second, make haste and invite the Lord into your home. How will you prepare to receive Him?

Simon Dewey

Come and See
THE FAITHFUL WITNESS

Help Thou Mine Unbelief

Without ceasing I make mention of you always in my prayers; . . .
for I long to see you, that I may impart unto you some spiritual gift,
to the end ye may be established; that is, that I may be comforted
together with you by the mutual faith both of you and me.

—Romans 1:9–12

A simple request. All I wanted was life. I never knew that we'd have to pray him here. But for those nine months I cried to the Lord for His blessing, day after day. And I'd say, *"As his mother, this burden is too hard to bear—what will it take?"*

He answered simply . . . faith.

I was fourteen weeks into my second pregnancy when I threatened to miscarry. After two trips to the emergency room and several more to the doctor, I was put on complete bed rest to try to save the baby's life.

Three days prior to my receiving this mandate, the bishop had come to our house to extend a calling for me to serve as the Relief Society president of our ward. Now, a week later, he was back, wondering how the Lord's inspiration fit in with this medical condition. As he sat on a chair next to my bed, he told me about the many trips he had taken to the temple that week, seeking direction from the Lord on proceeding with the call, and described the peaceful assurance he had felt that we should move forward. So I suggested to him the names of the sisters I wanted as my counselors, though I was unable even to show up for the sacrament meeting in which we would be sustained.

Later that week, I was set apart. The experience was one of the most powerful moments of my life. In the blessing, I was told that the baby would be born healthy, *if* I had enough faith and followed the direction of my doctor with exactness. I knew that I could follow the direction of my doctor, but the responsibility of having enough faith completely overwhelmed me. As soon as Greg and I were alone, I burst into tears. I couldn't do it. So much doubt crept into my mind daily that I knew I was not spiritually strong enough to have the faith to make the pregnancy succeed. I went to bed discouraged. Stuck in bed, I felt that I was unable to accomplish anything. I was failing as a wife, as a mother, and now as a Relief Society president. And to make matters worse, if the pregnancy failed, I would forever know that it was because of my lack of faith.

The day after I was set apart, I called a friend to ask for advice. As she had

"If thou canst believe, all things are possible to him that believeth."

—MARK 9:23

done on many previous occasions, she sent me to the scriptures to find my answer. I found myself in the ninth chapter of Mark, standing in the same shoes as the man who had come to the Savior, begging Jesus to heal his son, who was possessed of a "dumb spirit" (v. 17). The man explained that he had previously asked Jesus' disciples to heal his boy and they had been unable to do so. "But," he said, "if thou canst do any thing, have compassion on us, and help us" (v. 22).

Jesus had compassion on the man and his afflicted son and said: "If thou canst believe, all things are possible to him that believeth" (v. 23).

When I read those words, I immediately echoed the pleading of the father in my own heart. I felt quietly prompted that this man was not actually asking "*if* thou canst do any thing." He knew the Savior could, or he would not have come to Him. In my mind I heard instead the distraught father saying, *"Because you can do anything, have mercy on us."* And then I could hear the Savior say to me, not "*if* thou canst believe," because He knew that I was capable of believing in miracles—I had before, and if it

were not so, I would not have come to the place where I was at that time (see D&C 6:14). Instead, I heard this reply, *Because you can believe, all things are possible.*

Seeking the miracle, "the father of the child cried out, and said with tears, Lord, I believe; help thou mine unbelief" (Mark 9:24). Reading this, I instantly felt relief. The man was not perfect in his faith. He felt doubt, just as I had since moments after the priesthood blessing. But there was a difference. Willing to admit that his faith was not perfect, he offered everything he had and asked the Lord to make up what he lacked.

Here was the answer I needed. I was to plead not only for the healing to take place but also for the added faith I would need to *allow* the healing to take place.

And so it is in our everyday life. As we attend to difficulties, we can turn to the Savior. When we feel we are lacking as a mother, a wife, or a friend, we can rely on Him for answers. When we are not enough in our callings at church or in the many other areas in which we serve, we can look to Christ. And any time the task at hand seems more than we can bear, we can plead for His assistance. Then, "although our faith were only . . . the smallest, and the result to be achieved the greatest . . . nothing shall be impossible unto us. For all things are ours, if Christ is ours" (AE, Vol. II, 109).

Part of the promise of the Atonement is the blessing that comes after all we can do. When we are not enough, Christ can make up the difference. But we have to ask Heavenly Father, in the name of Christ, for the added strength. For drawing closer to Christ is not an event but a process. As we walk along that trail, we will find not only that Christ is aware of our limitations but that, after all we can do, He will compensate for them. The sense of falling short or falling down is a natural part of each of our lives. But we need to believe that after all we can do, Christ can fill that which is empty, straighten our bent parts, and make strong that which is weak. Never forget that the Lord is on our side (see Bruce C. Hafen, "Beauty for Ashes," *Ensign*, Apr. 1990, 85).

He can make us enough.

THE INVITATION . . . *Develop Faith*

Read the account of the pleading father in Mark 9:17–27.

THE JOURNEY

• Take time to identify and write down an area in which you feel you are not enough. This could include challenges that are physical, temporal, spiritual, or emotional.

• Take it to the Lord. Plead your case in prayer. Don't be afraid to acknowledge your weakness and ask for greater faith. Then be still and listen to the promptings that will come.

Simon Dewey

Come and See
THE FOUNT OF EVERY BLESSING

What Lack I Yet?

*Till thou hast paid
the very last mite.*

—LUKE 12:59

His suit was well worn and out of place with the crisp, sharp suits the other missionaries wore. But the boy did have one thing in common with the other elders; they had each arrived at the mission home for the first time. As the missionaries prepared to leave for their assigned areas, the mission president pulled the humble boy from South America aside and asked him where he had gotten his suit. He explained that his father had taken it off after church the Sunday before he left on his mission and had placed it in the small suitcase. Looking down, the mission president asked where the elder's weathered shoes had come from. The missionary replied that his father had taken them off his feet when they arrived at the airport and had given them to him just as he was ready to leave.

The boy's humble family had given all they had so this young man could serve the Lord.

Contrast this with the young man we read about in Mark 10. I imagine this boy was about the same age as the missionary. As Jesus was going forth, this rich young man came to speak to Him. We read that he came running and knelt at the Savior's feet. With seeming pure intent, he explained to the Lord that he had kept the commandments since he was a boy and now wanted to know what he needed to do additionally to inherit eternal life. He questioned the Lord, "What lack I yet?" (Matt. 19:20).

We can assume the question was sincere, for Mark tells us, "Jesus beholding him loved him" (Mark 10:21). The Lord then gave the boy specific counsel; but what He asked was not easy: "One thing thou lackest: go thy way, sell whatsoever thou hast, and give to the poor. . . and come, take up the cross, and follow me" (v. 21).

For the young man, the requirement was too great. Surrendering all he had was too much to ask, and rather than committing his all to the Savior, he "went away grieved" (v. 22).

The same might be true for many of us. Each must determine if he or she is willing to give up something of lesser value to obtain something of infinite value—whether to pay the price to "inherit eternal life" (v. 17).

How might we liken this story to our own lives? Do we willingly give all that we have to serve the Lord? It means more than just giving the visiting teaching message; it's being the friend. It means adding the final touches every time we serve in our callings. It means paying just a little more in our fast offerings, knowing that our small effort will make a significant difference to someone in need. It means getting out of our comfort zone to talk to someone new at church. It means remembering that "in the quiet heart is hidden sorrow that the eye can't see" (*Hymns*, no. 220) and learning to be less critical and more understanding. Sometimes it means giving up our seat, and other times it means giving up our entire afternoon. It means I'll be there, you can count on me, and I'm on your side. It means that we are always on the Lord's errand. It means that we are a true follower of Christ. Although it is hard to imagine at the time of our sacrifice, we receive, in the giving, something of far greater worth in its place.

There is a story found two chapters later in the same book of Mark that depicts this true devotion to the Lord. Interestingly, it seems that the woman in this story, who gave everything she had to the Lord, never met the Savior during His ministry on earth. Her reward was not immediate, but still, her devotion was sure.

I imagine Jesus sitting out of the way, watching the activity in the temple around Him. As He sat, "His gaze was riveted by a solitary figure. We can see her coming alone, as if ashamed to mingle with the crowd of rich givers. . . . She held in her hand only the smallest of coins, but it was all her living" (AE, Vol. II, 388). As Jesus watched, the woman threw in her two mites, giving every earthly thing she possessed to the Lord, without thought of recognition or reward, but in humble, quiet sacrifice. With great respect, Christ spoke of her to His disciples, saying, "This poor widow hath cast more in, than all they which have cast into the treasury: for all they did cast in of their abundance; but she *of her want* did cast in all that she had, even all her living" (Mark 12:43–44; emphasis added).

The scriptures do not define this woman's want. She may have wanted for food, shelter, or clothing. Perhaps she was following the commandment to pay her tithing and prove the Lord therewith, desiring the promised blessings she knew would follow. We do not know for certain, but we do know this: *of her want* she gave all she had.

I want to be like that.

THE INVITATION . . . *Give All*

Read the account of the rich young man in Mark 10:17–22 and the widow's mite in Mark 12:41–44.

THE JOURNEY

• Think of someone you know who has given all in service to the Lord. What lesson can you learn from that person? How can you be more like him or her?

• Commit today to give *all you have* in your service to the Lord. Choose one area where you feel you could give more. What changes will this require in your daily routines?

Simon Dewey

Come and See
THE ADVOCATE

After All

And there will I meet thee, and I will go before thee. . . .
And there will I bless thee. . . .
And thus I will do unto thee
because this long time ye have cried unto me.

—ETHER 1:42–43

It must have been frightening to be alive at the time when the Lord confounded the language of the people at the great tower. Imagine the confusion and panic as people were suddenly unable to speak or communicate with each other. Two brothers, worried for the welfare of their families, came up with a solution. Jared told his brother to cry unto the Lord that their language and the language of their families would not be confounded. The Lord heard their prayer and had compassion on them. He told the brother of Jared to gather his friends and families and all of their flocks and prepare to go to a land that was "choice above all the lands of the earth" (Ether 1:42).

The brother of Jared was commanded to build barges that would help the family reach their destination. The barges were built according to the instruction of the Lord. Because the brother of Jared was obedient at each step, he was able to receive the next level of knowledge. After the brother of Jared finished building the barges he reached a moment of indecision, questioning his next step. Knowing that he and his people would be spending a large amount of time traveling closed up inside the barges, he worried about two very significant problems: how would they breathe and what would they do about light?

Consider these two problems: one is an inconvenience, and one is a life-threatening situation. The brother of Jared took these problems to the Lord. A lesson can be learned from the way the Lord answered. The Lord did not want this group of people to perish. In answer to the humble pleading of a faithful servant to a question of immediate need the Lord answered directly. He gave a solution to the request for air, suggesting that the brother of Jared should make a hole in the top and in the bottom of the barges. When the people traveling in the barge needed air they were to unstop the hole and receive air, and when water began to come into the barge they were to stop up the hole again. A simple solution, and the brother of Jared did as the Lord had commanded.

"Ye receive no witness until after the trial of your faith."

—ETHER 12:6

Then he cried again unto the Lord, worried that there was no light in the barges, wondering if they were to cross the sea in darkness. The reply came quickly, just as it had with the first question, but the answer was entirely different. The Lord asked the brother of Jared, "What will ye that I should do that ye may have light in your vessels?" (Ether 2:23–25).

The brother of Jared did not sit and wait for a solution. He immediately went to work. He climbed up a mountain, and not just any mountain but a mountain of exceeding height, to find some stones. And he didn't take just any old stones, but rather he did "molten out of a rock sixteen small stones; and they were white and clear, even as transparent glass" (Ether 3:1) He did all the work he could do on his own, and *then* he cried unto the Lord.

The scriptures teach us, "Ye receive no witness until after the trial of your faith" (Ether 12:6). The brother of Jared faced a trial of faith, and his witness was twofold. The blessing came, the stones were touched and they received light. But more important than that is what happened in the process. As the Lord touched the stones, the mortal man saw the finger of the Lord. "And the brother of Jared fell down before the Lord, for he was struck with fear" (Ether 3:6). And the Lord said unto him, "Never has man come before me with such exceeding faith as thou hast" (Ether 3:9). Because of that exceeding faith, the Lord showed Himself to the brother of Jared, revealing, "Behold, I am he who was prepared from the foundation of the world to redeem my people. Behold, I am Jesus Christ. . . . Behold, this body, which ye now behold, is the body of my spirit; and man have I created after the body of my spirit; and even as I appear unto thee to be in the spirit will I appear unto my people in the flesh" (Ether 3:14, 16).

In verse 19 we are told that the brother of Jared had "faith no longer, for he knew, nothing doubting." He had received a witness; he had come to *know* the Lord.

After the Jaredites had prepared everything they needed for the voyage—their food, their flocks and herds, and everything they should carry with them—"they got aboard of their vessels or barges, and set forth into the sea, *commending themselves unto the Lord their God*. And it came to pass that the Lord God caused that there should be a furious wind blow upon the face of the waters, towards the promised land; and thus they were tossed upon the waves of the sea before the wind" (Ether 6:4–5; emphasis added).

I am always amazed at the faith of the Jaredites. How many of us would climb into a barge that we could not steer or direct in any way, to go to a destination we knew nothing about, and be willing to travel without even knowing how long the journey would take? And then, not only did they commend themselves to the Lord, the journey was not a calm one. Instead, furious winds blew them toward the promised land.

I love that even though the wind did never cease to blow, and the people were constantly driven, they sang praises unto the Lord. In the very midst of their adversity, they "did thank and praise the Lord all the day long; and when the night came, they did not cease to praise the Lord" (Ether 6:9). What a lesson of gratitude, of joy in the journey, of enduring to the end. When the Jaredites finally reached the promised land the first thing they did was bow themselves down upon the earth and "did shed tears of joy before the Lord, because of the multitude of his tender mercies over them" (Ether 6:12).

Have you received a blessing after all you could do?

Through the process did you come to know the Lord?

I was seventeen weeks into the pregnancy of our fourth child when I went into labor. Discouragement does not come close to describing the despair that encompassed me as I checked myself in to the women's center. After three hard pregnancies, I knew the odds were not good that we would keep this child. Any hope I might have had was dashed when the nurse who had been assigned to watch over me informed me that until twenty weeks of gestation this wouldn't be considered a viable pregnancy. There was nothing they would do to stop the contractions.

I had been extremely nauseous with this pregnancy, I had felt the baby growing inside me, and for the past week I had become aware of the initial kicking inside. I didn't know how anyone could fathom that this was not a viable pregnancy. After monitoring the baby and the contractions for two hours, the nurse confirmed my fears. I was contracting regularly. I begged her to call my doctor who knew my history to see if there was anything we could do. And then I began to pray. I prayed he would make the right decision—that we would try to save the tiny life that I had become fiercely attached to. And hope came. He put me on a medication to calm the contractions, and I was to stay down on complete bed rest. I went home and continued to pray.

My life consisted of constant bed rest, frequent baths to calm the contractions, weekly trips to the doctor, and a succession of priesthood blessings as we tried to cope with the magnitude of what we were facing. Finally, after four ultrasounds within three weeks, the doctor suggested there was one procedure we could try that could save the baby's life. This would do one of two things: it would either force me into hard labor, and I would deliver immediately, or it would slow down the damage being caused by the constant contractions. At twenty-one weeks it would be risky, but it was our only choice. To make matters worse, I would need to fast for twelve hours before the operation. This meant I could not take the medication I had been taking every two hours to calm the contractions. I was a nervous wreck. I remember lying on the operating table just before the surgery was to begin. I was completely exhausted. I had not slept soundly for weeks. It seemed that I had been using every muscle in my body to keep the baby inside. I hurt all over. I had done all I had been asked. I had given my best effort. We had fasted and prayed. We had called upon the Lord through the power of priesthood blessings. There was nothing more I could do. It was in the hands of my doctor. It was in the hands of the Lord. As I began to receive the anesthesia, I said the shortest prayer I had offered in the last four weeks, "Lord, thy will be done." I could do nothing more. It was out of my hands.

The first time I woke up in the recovery room I saw the anesthesiologist sitting next to me. Groggy and only halfway alert I asked the question pounding in my heart: "Did it work? Is the baby still alive? Am I still pregnant?" His answer was a simple yes. As I drifted back off to sleep I vividly heard a voice whisper in my head, "Thanks be unto God for his unspeakable gift." Later that day, I returned home to my familiar routine of complete bed rest. I was concerned that the contractions were not calming, but I was also intrigued by the whisper I had heard. I began to search the scriptures for the source of the simple message. The words had offered the first glimpse of hope I could cling to. The Spirit had spoken to my soul. I found the reference to my simple message in 2 Corinthians 9:15. For the first night in many weeks I slept in peace.

I spent almost six months in bed. Even up to the final week, the outcome was uncertain. As we walked into the delivery room the nurse asked if there was anything she could do to make our visit better. I told her, "Just deliver us a healthy baby, alive." She couldn't possibly understand the weight of that request. But Grace was born on September 21, healthy and full-term. My doctor couldn't believe it. As he pulled her out and laid her on my stomach, we admired every healthy bit of her from her tiny toes up to the curly white hair that covered her wrinkled head. "This is an angel baby," he told the nurses. "Look at this baby, and you'll see a miracle—you don't know what it took to get this one here."

My father told me to write it all down. He didn't want any of us to forget the miracle we had witnessed. We had also "seen the finger of the Lord" as He had brought Gracie to the earth. Just like the brother of Jared, my witness was also twofold. God had given me an unspeakable gift in my perfect baby daughter, but through the trial I also had come to know the Lord. The days that had turned into

"After the greatest trial comes the greatest gratitude."

weeks and months of doubt, discouragement, and despair had led me to call on the Lord for intercession, for help, and for comfort. I had come to know my Savior. I recognized His voice. I had felt His Spirit and His constant companionship as I struggled to go on. He had become real to me. I knew, nothing doubting.

In Ether 6:3 we read: "And thus the Lord caused stones to shine in darkness, to give light unto men, women, and children, that they might not cross the great waters in darkness." The Lord has promised each of us—men, women, and children—that He will not leave us to suffer in darkness or despair, He will send light to every one of us. As it says in Ether 2:25: "And behold, I prepare you against these things; for ye cannot cross this great deep save I prepare you against the waves of the sea, and the winds which have gone forth, and the floods which shall come." Isn't it interesting that the Lord told them they would not be able to face the task at hand unless He prepared a way for them? There comes a point in the midst of every trial when we submit to the will of the Lord. We give our best effort, and after all we can do, we lay the burden at His feet. We believe, we trust, and we allow Him to prepare a path for us toward the promised blessing.

Often we don't realize that the trial is what enables us to reach the destination the Lord has in mind for us. He will not let it destroy us, but He will let it move us in the direction we need to go. Just like the Jaredites, when we are encompassed about and in the depths of the trial, if we cry unto Him, He will bring us forth again.

After the greatest trial comes the greatest gratitude. I no longer question why we see so many pictures and read so many accounts depicting followers of Jesus who fall down at His feet in reverence when they meet Him. I imagine the weight of gratitude is so significant they cannot bear to stand in His presence; the gift He offers is unspeakable.

Faith is an unspeakable gift. It is the indescribable promise. It sustains the soul through moments that otherwise would destroy us. It is a gift that can be constantly replenished if we are willing. And the reward that awaits the true seeker is a treasure beyond compare.

If you are searching for your promised land, "seek this Jesus" (Ether 12:41), the One who encourages us to build, to perform great works, to prove ourselves worthy and obedient. Who offers solutions, who encourages us to search for ourselves and find the answers we long for. Seek this Jesus, who will not let you cross the water in darkness, who will prepare the way before you, who knows what you have been through, who knows what is still to come. The One who allows the trials because He knows the blessings that will follow. The One who will show you the greater things, who will bring the unspeakable gifts The One who leads us to the promise. "Seek this Jesus . . . that the grace of God the Father, and also the Lord Jesus Christ, and the Holy Ghost, which beareth record of them, may be and abide in you forever" (Ether 12:41).

THE INVITATION . . . *Understand Grace*

Read Ether 12 and look for the blessings.

THE JOURNEY

• Remember, grace comes after all you can do. Take time today to analyze a trying situation in your life. After you have done all that you can do, place it at the feet of the Lord. Keep a written record of the *greater things* and the *unspeakable gifts* that will come as He leads you to the promise.

Be Still

ৡৡ

Develop Faith

ৡৡ

Give All

ৡৡ

Understand Grace

Simon Dewey

Come and See
THE SAVIOR

Seek for More

Weeping may endure for a night,
but joy cometh in the morning.

—PSALM 30:5

The world around us is filled with discouragement. Adversity abounds, and in almost every home one can find a burden being shouldered. Like Lazarus, who lay dead in the enclosed tomb, we sometimes find ourselves surrounded by darkness. How often in the midst of our sorrow do we hear the voice of the Savior as He calls out with a loud voice, "Come forth" (John 11:43). Come forth from the darkness, despair, and discouragement that surround you, come forth from the sorrow and be healed.

In the midst of tribulation every soul takes a moment to ask why. Why me? Why now? What is the purpose for the anguish and the pain that I am experiencing? The mind searches for explanation; the heart questions its ability to withstand such intense emotion. In the search for a definite answer hope becomes dim and the struggle to simply exist takes over. It is hard to understand why bad things happen to good people. In these moments of despair we turn to God for answers. We become like the people of Alma: "And it came to pass that so great were their afflictions that they began to cry mightily to God" (Mosiah 24:10). We beg to understand the reason for the suffering.

We do not experience trials just to see if we will make it through. Each of us experiences the refiner's fire for one reason—to come to know the Refiner. We are not just tried; we are proven. Priceless lessons can be learned from the Master during times of adversity. It is in these moments of heartache that we come to know the Savior and more fully appreciate His atoning sacrifice. Lessons thus learned will prepare us to better endure what may follow and will sustain us through the darkest days of our lives.

Christ is always there. In the darkest hours of the night and the longest hours of the day, He is there. He is accessible and available at a moment's notice. His hope for us is taught in Hosea 5:15, where He says, "In their affliction they will seek me early." He knows that those who believe in Him will, in fact, prove Him. This process takes time, but in the end "a brother is born for adversity" (Prov. 17:17).

In the hours of suffering perhaps the greatest comfort comes in the realization that we are not alone. Christ has said, "Ye may know of a surety that I, the Lord God, do visit my people in their afflictions" (Mosiah 24:14). He will come to each of us. In our times of greatest trial He will visit, He will stand by us, and He will wait for us to acknowledge His presence and allow Him to intercede. Through the gift of the Atonement we will experience His healing power, if we but take the time to ask.

Mary Magdalene is a favored woman in the scriptures. She had the privilege of coming to know and love the Savior. Perhaps she was a dear friend, even a close confidant. We do not know much about Mary, but we do know that she was the first person to see the risen Lord. I have often wondered why.

Was her faith the most sufficient?

Was she the most prepared to receive the Savior?

Did Christ know she would recognize Him when He called her name because she had before?

For whatever reason she was thus favored, she went to the tomb early one morning after Christ had died, and here an important lesson was learned. She went seeking the Savior. In her hour of greatest need, in deep despair and longing for answers, she did what she had learned to do—she turned to Christ.

Arriving at the sepulchre and discovering the Lord's body was missing, she stood weeping outside the tomb. When she looked again into the empty crypt, she saw two angels in white, "And they say unto her, Woman, why weepest thou?" She replied, "Because they have taken away my Lord, and I know not where they have laid him." It was then "she turned herself back, and saw Jesus standing, [but] knew not that it was Jesus" (John 20:13–14). He also asked her, "Woman, why

weepest thou? Whom seekest thou?" (v. 15). She supposed the man to be the gardener, and it was only when He spoke her name that she recognized the resurrected Lord.

Mary was a woman who had a great level of knowledge of the teachings of Christ. She lived on the earth and really knew the Savior during His ministry. Yet still, she did not at first recognize Him.

On that Easter morning Mary's level of understanding was that Christ was dead. Weeping in frustration and sorrow, she sought to find Him. She did not recognize His voice at first because in her mind it was not possible. But then—it was! Mary's testimony of Christ increased. She had reached a new level of understanding.

How often do we come to a point in our lives when we are comfortable and confident in our relationship with Christ? We may go forward for a time serving and learning. Inevitably a trial will come that will test our knowledge. We may question our trust in the reality of the Lord. At these times we realize that our testimony is never stagnant. Trials provide an opportunity for us to seek the Savior. As we prove Him, we gain more understanding and knowledge.

Mary did not recognize the Savior until He called her name. Then, suddenly, light and understanding came. A new level of knowledge: Christ was risen; He lives; there is life after death. He had triumphed and was victorious. The Savior stood by her in her moment of learning. He waited patiently until she was ready, and then He taught.

Do we recognize the voice of the Lord? We can prepare to hear His voice by reading our scriptures, remembering to pray, keeping the commandments, and attending the temple. But even when we are regularly doing these things there will be times when our faith is tried. We will plead for greater understanding. And perhaps as Mary did, we will weep. It is at such times, when we are downtrodden enough to find ourselves humbly pleading, as Mary was, that we will recognize the voice of the Savior. Our understanding will be increased, and we will be led out of darkness into light. Then we will celebrate with great joy in praise of the Lord. He will know when we are ready for the lesson because He knows our hearts.

Through every trial our faith is tested. Sometimes faith precedes the miracle. Other times we must have faith to trust in God's will. At both of these times our spirit seems to be stretched to the limit as we learn, line upon line, how faith works. When we find ourselves asking, *Where is the promise, where is the reason for this pain, and where do I turn now?* I hope we will follow the example of Mary and go to Christ, for He is the greatest Healer, the Healer of all wounds.

THE INVITATION . . . *Seek*

Read the account of Mary Magdalene in John 20:1–18.

THE JOURNEY

• Examine your life. What is your greatest need?

• Sometime today find a way to seek the Lord. Find in Christ the answers you long for. Dare to reach a new level of understanding.

Come and See
THE FRIEND

Art Thou Only a Stranger?

And it came to pass that I
. . . having great desires to know
. . . did cry unto the Lord;
and behold he did visit me.

—1 Nephi 2:16

Three days before our wedding, my soon-to-be husband, Greg, went to an Instacare medical clinic because he had a sore throat and the beginnings of a head cold. During the examination the doctor informed us that he could feel a tumor on Greg's thyroid. Worried that it might be cancerous, he suggested Greg have an additional examination as soon as we arrived home from our honeymoon. We did so. Greg saw a specialist at the University of Utah Medical Center, and the findings were not good. The biopsy revealed that there was a ninety-seven percent chance of the tumor being malignant, and we were terrified. Within six weeks, Greg was scheduled for surgery.

Change is never easy, and facing something of this magnitude so early in our marriage scared us both. Following the surgery, I sat alone next to Greg's bed in the hospital room. My parents lived out of town, and Greg's parents had gone home for the night. Greg was heavily sedated, and I found myself sitting in that dark room in the middle of the night completely alone with my thoughts. Sometimes loneliness is frightening. I tried to hold on to all that was familiar, to all of the dreams that we had planned. And in the depths of my heart I wished that there could have been someone who would sustain me and stay the night with me.

Never before in my life had I been faced with a trial that depleted all of my reserves as this one had. Over time, I would come to know that that God would hold me in the palm of His hand. But that understanding didn't come immediately. I was beginning to realize that sometimes it has to hurt to make you strong, and in the days that followed, I took comfort in the words of familiar verses of scripture: "Draw near unto me and I will draw near unto you" (D&C 88:63); "My peace I give unto you" (John 14:27); "Be still and know that I am God" (D&C 101:16). These whispered messages from the Lord became my greatest comfort. Although it would take months for Greg to return to full health, which he did, I had begun the most important journey of my life—my own road to Emmaus, where I would come to know and recognize the Savior.

"Be still and know that I am God."

—D&C 101:16

Imagine being with the two unnamed disciples who left the city in the early afternoon of one spring day. We would walk for almost an hour, passing country houses along the way. Beyond a dreary, rocky region, we would climb a path with streams running alongside. We would pass orchards of orange and lemon trees, olive groves, and shady nooks. In all, our walk would encompass almost six or seven miles, and every mile of it would be filled with talk of Jesus Christ, the disciples each sharing memories, tinged with sadness because of His recent passing and the mystery of the empty tomb (see AE, Vol. II, 639).

Somewhere in our journey, a stranger would join us on the road, but caught up in conversation we would not at first recognize Him. After inquiring about the source of our sorrow, the stranger would then begin to expound to us the scriptures that pertained to the coming of the Messiah. By now it would almost be evening, the day far spent, and reaching our destination, the disciples would invite us and the stranger to tarry with them. And while partaking of a simple meal, the eyes of our understanding would be opened, and we would recognize the resurrected Lord before He suddenly vanishes from our sight.

Imagine our wonder, expressed by one of those disciples: "Did not our heart burn within us, while he talked with us by the way, and while he opened to us the scriptures?" (Luke 24:32; see vv. 13–32).

Often we walk our own road to Emmaus, so consumed by life's demands that it is hard for us to open our eyes to the miracles that surround us. If we are able to recognize our spiritual longing, we might be moved to plead: "O Savior, stay this night with me; Behold, 'tis eventide" (*Hymns*, no. 165).

And He *will* abide with us. We can draw nearer to Christ by reading the scriptures. If we do not take the opportunity to read the words of the Lord daily, we may fail to recognize the Master who accompanies us along the journey. How sad it

"O Savior, stay this night with me; Behold, 'tis eventide."

—*Hymns, no. 165*

would be to arrive at the end of the journey and realize we never came to know the Visitor with whom we have traveled.

For we do not travel alone. We have been given the same promise that was given the disciples: "In the silence of our hearts, if only we crave for it, and if we walk with Him, He sometimes so opens from the Scriptures . . . the things concerning Himself" (AE, Vol. I, 642).

There have been many evenings, as the shadows have fallen around me, when I have turned to the scriptures for comfort. In those quiet moments, just like the unnamed disciples, I have found verses that have caused *my* heart to burn within *me*. Often, those whispered assurances from the Lord have been just what I have needed to sustain and lift me and carry me through. Great blessings will come

"In the silence of our hearts, if only we crave

for it, and if we walk with Him, He

sometimes so opens from the Scriptures . . .

the things concerning Himself."

—ALFRED EDERSHEIM

if we learn to acknowledge the presence of the Savior along this journey of life. As we turn to the scriptures and begin to recognize the voice of the Lord, there will be moments when our hearts will burn within us. These moments will teach us to look to Him more often. "When other helpers fail and comforts flee" we will instinctively cry out: "Help of the helpless, oh, abide with me!" (*Hymns*, no. 166).

The Invitation . . . *Abide*

Read the account of the disciples walking on the road to Emmaus, found in Luke 24:13–32.

The Journey

- Learn to use the scriptures to receive personal revelation from the Lord.
- Take some time today to find a scripture that speaks to you.
- Let His Spirit abide in your heart by reflecting on that scripture throughout the day.

Come and See

THE DELIVERER

What Mean These Stones?

Take you hence
. . . twelve stones.

—JOSHUA 4:3

One early March I traveled with a group of about sixty fifth-grade boys to Clear Creek Camp located up Spanish Fork Canyon. Shortly after we arrived, the principal of the school informed us that we would be taking a two-mile hike through nearly three feet of fresh snow. When we left the valley there had been no snow on the ground, and many of the boys did not think to bring boots. However, we were all required to make the trek, so we were told to dress as warmly as we could.

The hike proved to be exciting, as excursions usually are with eleven-year-old boys. Within the first hour we stopped to discuss wildlife and the difference between deciduous and coniferous trees and paused to climb a twenty-foot, hand-made wall.

As we were beginning the last half of the hike, I noticed the boy in front of me was missing a shoe. We searched all around but could not find it anywhere. The scary thing was his foot was so numb with cold that he hadn't even realized he had lost the shoe, and he had no idea how long it had been missing.

As a mother, I was worried, and we decided that the boy should put on both of my boots, because his feet were so wet and frozen. I resorted to the next best thing. Each of the boys had been asked to bring a large plastic garbage bag on the hike, so I put two bags on over my socks and then pulled his wet socks over the top of the bags to keep them in place. Once we had made the switch we began to hike again through the snow.

The principal had passed us in the process of switching boots and was fully aware of the situation, so it really surprised me when he directed us to continue up the mountain instead of returning home. Since we had been hiking for more than an hour, I didn't want to turn back alone, and so I followed. I made it for about five minutes before the cold started to sink in. With the use of a pair of snowshoes I was able to keep from sinking, but my feet still came in direct contact with the snow with every step. I was freezing, and still we were making our way *up* the hill.

I tried thinking of the pioneers to convince myself that this sacrifice was minimal compared to what they must have walked through, but that lasted only about fifteen minutes, and then I was fighting back tears and frustration. I wondered what the principal was thinking. By the time we finally stopped our climb, I realized we were more than an hour from our cars by the way we had come, and I knew I wasn't going to make it back; I was pretty sure they would have to send in a helicopter to rescue me. I looked with some irritation at the principal, who was now explaining to the boys why some of the trees on the mountain had grown in the valleys and why some areas had no trees at all. We were standing almost at the crest, with the mountain falling below us at a steep angle, and far below us, I could see our three cabins nestled in the trees. By now I was standing on my heels to keep the rest of my feet out of the snow, and I wondered how I would ever get back. I figured the principal had forgotten about me. Surely he must have, or he would have raced us all home the way we had come.

Then, just when I thought I couldn't take it any longer, the principal did the strangest thing. He lay down flat on his back on one of the large plastic bags and began sliding down the hill, full speed toward the cabins. The rest of us were shocked! And then it dawned on us what he was doing. This was the purpose of the plastic bags. We were to sit on them and slide home.

I have never been so grateful for a plastic garbage bag in my life! I sat down and started sliding and found myself back at the cabins within ten minutes. I had made it! And I realized that all along the principal had known what he was doing. He knew I would be fine, because he knew the plan, and he had prepared the quickest way to get me out of a tough situation.

In a small way, this experience reminds me of how many scripture stories testify to the fact that the Savior truly does deliver His people. Think of Moses and the Red Sea, Noah and the flood, or the people of Alma who were in bondage for so many years. History proves the love the Lord has for His people and His willingness and ability to lead them to a promised land. The power of God is amazing. The scriptures provide countless examples of times when the Lord stretched forth His hand to offer relief for His children who were struggling. In every dispensation

"History proves the love the Lord has for His people and His willingness and ability to lead them to a promised land."

He has provided miracles for His children as they have wandered through the wilderness toward a better life. They have proved the Lord, and He has been there.

A favorite poem reads:

> *When you come to the Red Sea place in your life*
> *In spite of all you can do*
> *There is no way back, there is no way round*
> *There is no way but through*
> *Then know God with a soul serene*
> *And the dark and the storm are gone*
> *God stills the wind*
> *God stills the waves*
> *God says to your soul "Go on"*

> —BAIRD T. SPALDING

Many years after Moses and his people experienced the miracle of crossing the Red Sea on dry ground, Joshua found himself in much the same situation, required to lead the Lord's people across a great river to the other side. As the people gathered to ford the river Jordan, Joshua promised them in the name of the Lord that the Lord would gather all the water into a "heap" and told them that they would be able to cross on dry ground. Joshua assured the people that the Lord, *without fail*, would provide their need (see Josh. 3:10–13).

As that miracle occurred, the Lord instructed Joshua to have twelve men each haul "upon his shoulder" a stone from the riverbed, to be used to erect a monument to the event on the other side of Jordan (see Josh. 4:5–7).

I imagine that making the crossing was quite a task. These twelve men probably had families, young children, cattle, and personal belongings they were required to move across this great riverbed. Now, as if they were not shouldering enough, they were asked to add more weight to their load. As they experienced this added burden, some may have questioned the Lord: *Could we not set up a monument with stones from the far side of the river and still remember the journey?* What was the purpose of the extra burden?

Once they reached the other side of the river, Joshua had the twelve stones placed together as a memorial. "And he spake unto the children of Israel, saying, When your children shall ask their fathers in time to come, saying, What mean these stones? Then ye shall let your children know, saying, Israel came over this Jordan on dry land. . . . That all the people of the earth might know the hand of the Lord, that it is mighty" (Josh. 4:21–24). These twelve men left a legacy to their families for generations to come of their testimony of the Lord and the great power He has to bless His people.

We also can leave a legacy for our families. One of the ways we can do this is to have visual reminders in our homes that testify of Jesus Christ. These might include statues, paintings, or framed scriptures. We once had a stake president who suggested that each of our children hang a picture of the Savior in his or her bedroom. Then he added a second, very important piece of counsel: this picture should represent the way they view the Savior. We spent an entire month helping our children find paintings that were just right. Each chose something different—the paintings each reflecting their personal testimony of what the Savior means to them.

Another way we can leave a legacy is through bearing our testimonies of the ways the Lord has touched our lives. These written or spoken declarations can serve to encourage those who are dear to us to recognize the hand of the Lord in their own lives. Share your testimony of Christ today with someone who is dear to you. There are many ways that you can do that; it might be through a letter or in a conversation. Find a way that is meaningful to you.

Experience has taught me that throughout the journey, the faithful traveler holds close to his heart the hope of reaching a promised land. In this case, the "promised land" we are searching for is a greater awareness and a stronger testimony of Christ. By drawing closer to Him we will be able to reach that destination. If our heart is willing He will *without fail* lead us to where we want to be.

"He knows the way because He *is* the way"(Jeffrey R. Holland, "Broken Things to Mend," *Ensign*, May 2006, 71; emphasis in original).

THE INVITATION . . . *Remember*

Read the story of Joshua and the crossing of the river Jordan in Joshua 3 and 4.

THE JOURNEY

• Either figuratively or literally, gather twelve stones. Assign each stone to represent a blessing that you have recognized in your journey toward Christ.

• Share these blessings with your family. Testify how you are coming to know the Healer, the Master, the Son of God, even Jesus Christ. What are the stories you can tell about how He has strengthened, enlightened, comforted, or otherwise blessed you?

SEEK

~~

ABIDE

~~

REMEMBER

The Celebration

Hang on the walls of your mind the memory of your successes. Take counsel of your strength, not your weakness. Think of the good jobs you have done. Think of the times when you rose above your average level of performance and carried out an idea or a dream for which you had deeply longed. Hang these pictures on the walls of your mind and look at them as you travel the roadway of life.

—Attributed to Whistler by Sterling W. Sill, "Great Experiences," *Ensign*, June 1971, 43.

I love celebrations that include each guest receiving a favor. Often this favor comes wrapped in a clear cellophane bag containing small treasures that have something to do with the theme of the party. As you go home you carry with you a tangible memory. Each time you look at one of those small treasures you are reminded of the celebration.

Think of this chapter as your own favor—a way for you to carry with you a memory of your journey. The best way to capture lessons learned is to write them down. Then, when we have moments when we need strength, guidance, or direction, we can look back to times in our lives when we have been blessed with those gifts.

Find a quiet time to reflect on the past twenty-one days. Read your journal entries. As you do, note the treasures you have found and the discoveries you have made. Have any of those experiences helped you to see more clearly the hand of the Lord in your life? Pause to reflect on the lessons you have learned. Have you felt joy, peace, strength, or understanding? What are the moments when you have felt closer to Christ?

Recalling the treasures and celebrations experienced along this journey closer to Christ will provide you with a lasting reminder to turn to Him in times of future need.

I have never enjoyed good-byes, or any type of endings for that matter, so I am thrilled that this is not the end of our journey. These twenty-one days have only been the beginning of a journey closer to Christ that can last forever. A Chinese proverb wisely counsels, "The journey *is* the reward." I hope you have found that to be true. In the days to come may your on-going search be constant. Consider the rising of the sun every morning as a personal invitation to make the most of each new day—an invitation to know and recognize the hand of the Lord in your life—an invitation to *come and see,* to continue the personal journey that will bring you closer to Christ. Respond, if you please.

How great reason have we to rejoice;

for could we have supposed when we started …

that God would have granted unto us such great blessings?

And now, I ask, what great blessings

has he bestowed upon us?

Can ye tell?

—ALMA 26:1–2

INDEX